THE BIRTH OF THE MOVIES

THE
BIRTH OF THE
MOVIES

D. J. Wenden

E. P. DUTTON · NEW YORK

First published 1975 by E. P. Dutton & Co., Inc.
All rights reserved.

© 1974 by D. J. Wenden

ISBN   0 525 47394 7

Printed in Great Britain

CONTENTS

For Eileen, with whom I have been
going to the pictures for thirty-five years

PREFACE

This book grew out of a series of documentary and feature films shown to history students at Oxford in the 1960s. Together with Dr J. M. Roberts, Fellow and Tutor of Modern History at Merton College, Oxford, I selected films illustrating historical events and movements of interest to historians and gave lectures suggesting how they could be understood and interpreted. In preparing these lectures we soon discovered that while there are many books about motion pictures as an art form, many studies of directors and several good general histories of the cinema (especially by French authors), there are few books which examine the subject from the standpoint of a historian interested in 20th-century political, economic and social changes as well as in developments within the film industry itself. Experience of teaching modern European history for twenty-five years, together with a passion for the movies lasting over forty years, prompted me to try to write a general introduction to the story of the motion picture from 1895 to 1927 as a historian sees it.

The Birth of the Movies seeks to explain how the cinema developed in this period and how it influenced social, economic and political events in Europe and America. The book may also explain to students of the cinema how the industry, the stars, directors and their financial backers were controlled by larger economic and political forces outside the studios. Much of the background is still obscure. Film history is notoriously a mixture of fact, fantasy and gossip. Dedicated scholars, most notably Dr Rachael Low in this country, are beginning to sift the evidence and produce definitive versions of some periods and topics. *The Birth of the Movies* does not claim to solve any of the major problems, but by building on the work of earlier authors and on the experience of countless hours of film viewing, it suggests an interpretation of certain features in the early story of the cinema and suggests areas which could profitably be explored in depth.

The first three chapters outline the main events in the evolution of the cinema from the Lumière brothers to Al Jolson. Chapters 4, 5 and 6 seek to examine its economic, social and political implications. Chapter 7 discusses the remarkable domination of a world industry by one small area generally described as Hollywood. The final chapter explains how the 'talkies' took over from the silent cinema and changed the nature of the art and the business.

If this book encourages historians to look at old films as material for the understanding of the 20th century and encourages movie enthusiasts to relate the pictures on the screen to the society which created them it will have done its job.

I am indebted in particular to the stills department of the British Film Institute for their help in supplying the vast majority of illustrations that appear in the book. The photographs on pages 14, 18 (bottom), 20, 42 (top right), 44 (bottom), 48, 56, 84, 93, 98 (bottom), 99, 114, 121 (top and bottom right), 125, 132, 133, 138 (top), 146 (top left) and 158 are reproduced by courtesy of the Radio Times Hulton Picture Library, and the photograph on page 109 (bottom) by kind permission of Oxford City Libraries.

I would like to thank Lisa Pontecorvo, who knows almost more about early 20th-century documentary films than the men who made them, for all her assistance, and Mrs Sandra Oatham and Mrs Mayling Stubbs who typed the manuscript.

D.J.W.
Oxford, June 1973

CHAPTER ONE

The primitive days of cinema

Most early film-makers entered the industry by chance. George Pearson has described his first experience of moving pictures in Lambeth Walk, London, at the beginning of the century. Outside a derelict greengrocer's shop 'a hawkeyed gentleman on a fruit crate was bewildering a sceptical crowd...there was a miracle to be seen for a penny, but only twenty-four could enter at a time, there wasn't room for more...you've seen pictures of people in books, all frozen stiff...you've never seen pictures with people coming alive, moving about like you and me.' Pearson describes how he paid his penny and joined twenty-three other sceptics inside.

Stale cabbage leaves and a smell of dry mud gave atmosphere to a scene from Hogarth. A furtive youth did things to a tin oven on iron legs and a white sheet swung from the ceiling ... Suddenly things happened ... the tin apparatus burst into a fearful clatter and an oblong picture was slapped on the white sheet and began a violent dance. After a while I discovered it was a picture of a house, but a house on fire. Flames and smoke belched from the windows, and – miracle of miracles – a fire engine dashed in, someone mounted a fire escape, little human figures darted out below and then ... Bang! The show was over. Exactly one minute and I had been to the cinema.[1]

George Pearson went again and again. A few years later, at the age of thirty-seven, he was both acting in and directing his own films. In 1929 he directed a British film with British actors in Hollywood. It is unlikely that any of his twenty-three companions in the greengrocer's shop became film actors, directors or script writers, but most of them probably became film 'fans'. They joined the vast cinema audiences of the 1920s and 1930s who crowded into the ornate palaces of that era – the Roxy in New York with its luxurious seating for 6250 people, Green's Playhouse in Glasgow with room for 4400, the Gaumont Palace, the largest in Europe, with seats for 6000 Parisians, and the Universum on the Kurfürstendamm in Berlin, designed by Erich Mendelsohn under the influence of the German Bauhaus school of architecture. By 1929 movie audiences in the United States alone totalled over 90 million a week: the industry was America's fourth largest, and one of the most profitable. The first major talking picture, *The Jazz Singer* (1927), made for Warner Brothers a profit of two million dollars on their 500,000-dollar outlay; Cecil Hepworth's renowned *Rescued by Rover,* made in England in 1905, had cost less than eight pounds, or about twenty dollars. Costs rose astronomically, but so did the value of the prizes to be won.

Motion pictures did not appear fully fledged on one specific day as the result of the work of one single inventor. On the side of Macy's store on 34th Street in New York a bronze plaque states: 'Here the Motion Picture began. At this site, on the night of 23 April, 1896 at Koster and Bial's Music Hall, Thomas A. Edison's motion pictures were projected.' The 23 April may be Shakespeare's birthday but it is not indisputably the birthday of the projected motion picture show. On 1 November 1895 two German showmen, Max and Emil Skladanowsky, demonstrated their Bioscope in a variety programme at the Berlin Wintergarten. Short films were screened of traditional dancing by children, two kangaroos boxing, and similar novelties. Their machine showed only very short circular films of repeated movements. It was never developed, although the name lingers on in South Africa where people still talk of 'going to the Bioscope' when they visit the cinema.

The first successful performance in front of a paying audience was given by the Lumière family to thirty-three customers at the Salon Indien of the Grand Café, 14 Boulevard des Capucines, Paris, on 28 December 1895. The programme of ten short films lasted only twenty minutes in all. One of the most famous sequences is *La Sortie des Usines,* a film of Lumière's work-people leaving his factory in the Rue Saint-Victor in Lyons. That street has now been renamed 'Rue du Premier-Film' – the Street of the First Film. These films had been shown privately earlier in the year, as had those of an Englishman, Birt Acres, who had

Louis Lumière (right) being congratulated by Walt Disney during the 40th anniversary celebrations of his first film show. Both the Lumière brothers lived well on into the talkie era

Birt Acres, one of the first English film pioneers

filmed the 1895 Oxford-Cambridge Boat Race and the opening of the Kiel Canal by Kaiser Wilhelm II, and who later showed a comedy, *Golfing Extraordinary*, in which 'one gentleman in attempting to strike the ball, misses, and falls headlong, much to the amusement of the bystanders'.[2]

All these shows included the essential features of the silent cinema: a series of photographs taken in succession that could be projected rapidly one after another to create the illusion of movement on the screen. They could entertain the thirty-three onlookers present at the first Lumière show or the crowd of 25,000 which looked at the giant screen erected for the Paris Exhibition of 1900, the forerunner of the open air drive-in movies. The simultaneous successes of 1895–6 were the climax of a period of experimentation in which attempts had been made to combine the features of mechanical moving pictures, the magic lantern projector and camera images.

The camera and the photographic reproduction of real life scenes had appeared in the mid-19th century. In 1884 cameras were used by an English photographer Edward Muybridge (Muggeridge before he emigrated from Kingston, Surrey, to America) to capture the moving action of a racehorse for his patron, Leland Stanford, the Californian railroad millionaire and founder of Stanford University. Stanford bet his friends that when a horse galloped all four of its legs were at some time off the ground simultaneously. Muybridge was employed to produce photographic proof. He placed a series of cameras in a line at short intervals apart. As a horse raced past its hooves snapped trip wires connected to the shutters of the cameras. The series of pictures secured the stake money for Stanford but did not produce a satisfactory moving picture. When the photographs were placed on a wheel and revolved, the horse's legs moved but the animal appeared to be galloping on the spot.

These photographs were captured on glass plates by twenty-four separate cameras. No one piece of equipment could take multiple pictures in rapid succession until the introduction of flexible film on paper, made possible by the transfer of photographic emulsion on to a celluloid base. This process was discovered by Hannibal Goodwin, a parson in Newark, New Jersey, in 1887, and patented by George Eastman, a local photographic manufacturer. The Eastman Kodak Company sold cameras and films in every continent and Eastman became a multi-millionaire. His largest donation to charity went not to an organization associated with the industry that had made his fortune but to found the Eastman Dental Centre at the University of Rochester. This new film was used by an Englishman, William Friese Greene, in his attempts to create a movie camera and to project its pictures on to a screen. His experiments were never completely successful, and the first satisfactory movie camera emerged from the Thomas Edison Laboratories in West Orange, New Jersey, birthplace of a dazzling series of electrical and mechanical inventions and developments, in-

William Friese Greene (1855–1921), an early experimenter who died at a public meeting designed to encourage the British motion picture industry

cluding the ticker tape, the telegraph, telephone, electric light bulb, typewriter and phonograph. Edison's research team, led by an Englishman, W. K. Laurie Dickson, produced the movie camera in 1889. Five years later they had perfected the Kinetoscope. This large wooden box had a peep-hole at the top through which a paying customer could view Mr Edison's moving pictures, like the primitive machines still surviving on some English seaside piers and showing *What the Butler Saw*.

Edison's films were made at his West Orange studio, an oddly shaped room of wood and canvas without windows. The room was mounted on a turntable base which could be revolved to follow the sun and direct its bright rays through a skylight onto the actors enclosed below. This contraption was called 'The Black Maria'. From it emerged short films of simple movements, men dancing, sneezing, playing the fiddle, and the first outrageous screen kiss of May Irwin and John Rice in 1896. Sometimes the camera was taken out of the studio to photograph street scenes, railway trains or public events.

These, and similar films photographed by the Lumière brothers, were projected onto the screen in 1895–6 and were

'The Black Maria' in which early Edison films were made

seen by as many as one hundred customers simultaneously instead of the limited audiences in the Kinetoscope saloons. There were no great dramas, no film stars, no rapid cross-cutting of images to heighten tension, no custard pies or chases. For the first audiences the novelty of movement on the screen was enough in itself. They cried out as the train entered the station towards them, mercifully stopping in time, or jumped back to avoid the splashing waves at the foot of Dover Cliffs. Even the great Russian novelist Maxim Gorky was surprised by the realism of Lumière's *Watering the Gardener* and wrote: 'You think the spray is going to hit you too and you instinctively shrink back.'[3] Gorky had visited a Lumière show at the Nizhni-Novgorod Fair in July 1896 and his review for the local newspaper began: 'Last night I was in the Kingdom of the Shadows.'[4] The Kingdom of the Shadows appeared at fairs and music-hall shows throughout Europe and America and as far afield as Bombay. Crowned heads marvelled at the new diversion; performances were given for Emperor Francis Joseph of Austria, the Kings of Sweden and Romania, the Queen of Spain, and in 1897 at Windsor Palace for the aged Queen Victoria. A year later another novelist, Henry James, paid a visit to 'the cinematograph, or whatever they call it'[5] and was impressed, and six years later Rudyard Kipling used a film sequence of a train arriving at Paddington Station as the key feature in his strangest short story, 'Mrs Bathurst'.

Edison took inadequate steps to protect his team's invention. He took out only American patent rights for his camera and projector. He had been too interested in his ultimate objective, the synchronization of moving pictures with the sound from his other invention, the phonograph, to appreciate the full value of the equipment he had already produced. Later attempts to suppress competition from other film-makers were handicapped by an initial failure to foresee the potential value of the camera and projector even without a recorded sound accompaniment.

Two of his assistants, W. K. Laurie Dickson and Eugene Lauste, broke away from Edison, patented their own inventions, and formed the American Mutoscope and Biograph Company. They were backed by William McKinley, then Governor of Ohio and later President of the United States. They adopted his Republican slogan as their company's motto, 'America for the Americans', and in 1897 were able to take advantage of the heavy tariffs imposed in the Dingley Tariff Act to drive Lumière's agent out of America. But no individual or company could monopolize the new invention. The techniques and patents were too widely spread. By 1900 scores of companies were operating in America and throughout Europe, turning out short travel or anecdotal films limited to fifty feet (the longest length of film available) as a novelty turn for vaudeville shows or for showmen travelling round fairs and markets. Typical of the material of these early films was *Egg and Spoon Race for Lady Cyclists* made by Cecil Hepworth in England. The catalogue says: 'At a signal a bevy of ladies ride in on their bicycles, dismount at the line of eggs, and commence the difficult task of picking them up in the spoons with which each lady is provided. They then remount with one hand while holding the egg balanced in the other, and ride on to the winning post.'[6]

The two men who played the next important role in the history of the movies were not inventors and technicians like Edison, Dickson and the Lumière Brothers, but the artists and film-makers Georges Méliès and Edwin Porter. Méliès came from the theatre into the movies. He was also a mechanic and a conjuror. He used these talents to extend the range of the cinema, taking it beyond the simple filmed episodes and travelogues produced up to 1900, into the more ambitious realm of a narrative cinema which told complicated stories and began to develop as an art form in its own right.

At an early stage Méliès approached his fellow Frenchman Lumière and asked if he could buy a camera. Lumière refused: 'Young man, you should be grateful, since although my invention is not for sale, it would undoubtedly ruin you. It can be exploited for a certain time as a scientific curiosity but, apart from that, it has no commercial future whatsoever.'[7] Méliès was not convinced, bought a camera from Georges Demeny, and went on to make hundreds of films between 1896 and 1914. Lumière's prophecy, however, was ultimately fulfilled, for Méliès died almost penniless in 1938 in a variety artists' home, having seen many of his best films ruthlessly pirated by American copyists.

Méliès, in his studio at Montreuil, combined the skills of magician and trick cameraman to produce fantasy and adventure films which told intricate stories in a style which only the cinema could produce. People disappeared mysteriously, strange ghost-like apparitions emerged, animals changed into human beings and flew through the air. Méliès developed the technical tricks of the camera: fast and slow motion, fade-outs, dissolves from one image to another, double or multiple exposure (which enabled one man – Méliès himself – to represent all the players in a band), and incorporated them into films that ran as long as twenty minutes and showed a succession of different scenes, a development from the short one-sequence novelties of 1895–6. His most famous film, *A Trip to the Moon* (1902), is half way between the science fiction of Jules Verne and the televised lunar exploration of Neil Armstrong in 1969. He showed the astronauts planning the trip, constructing a projectile, being shot off to the moon, landing in the eye of the man in the moon (causing it to weep a large tear), descending into a lunar crater, being attacked by the Selenite inhabitants, fleeing from the moon, splashing down in the open sea, and sinking to the bottom of the ocean. The film ended with their ultimate retrieval and triumphant processional parade.

Georges Méliès' version of A Trip to the Moon

A fantasy transformation scene from a Méliès film with a typically theatrical décor

Scene from an early Méliès film in which he ridicules a pacifist conference. The meeting breaks up in disorder as the peace-loving delegates assault each other

John Williamson's studio and film works at Hove, near Brighton

Méliès' style and technical skills were widely copied. At Hove in Sussex, John A. Williamson made an early British comedy, *The Clown Barber*: a barber distracted by a fidgety customer cuts off the man's head and places it on a table; having completed the shave, he replaces the head and the satisfied customer pays and walks out of the saloon. But Méliès became trapped in his own theatrical style. After his early outdoor street scenes he concentrated on interior studio productions with stage settings. His plots were drawn from the world of pantomime and illusion and he rarely attempted any theme drawn from real life. The people in his films were performers, not characters. He made little attempt to use the cinema's ability to create an illusion of reality, to make the audience believe that they were watching actual events photographed by chance, rather than enjoying a fantasy obviously staged for their entertainment. For filmgoers in the first decade of the 20th century the contrast between the romances of Méliès and the realistic stories of Edwin Porter or a contemporary English film such as *The Life of Charles Peace* must have been as sharp as the contrast for us between

Preparing a trick sequence for Le Bon Ecraseur, *1908*

a 1970s ciné-verité movie, shot almost entirely on location, and the Hollywood films of the 1930s with their obvious studio sets and heroines whose coiffure and make-up remain undisturbed no matter what extremes of emotional or climatic stress they endure. Méliès stamped the theatrical mark on some of his films by lining up his performers at the end of the reel to take a curtain call as if they were appearing on the stage.

The next great pioneer, Edwin S. Porter, a Scotsman who had settled in America, had no theatrical experience. He began as a cameraman and mechanic. He was a camera assistant for the first Edison show at Koster and Bial's in 1896. The following year he set up a business with W. J. Beadnell to manufacture cameras and projectors. After his premises had been destroyed by fire in 1900, he returned to film-making. The disaster may have given him the idea for his first famous movie, *The Life of an American Fireman* (1902).

Porter's films were realistic and he broke away from the conventions of the theatre. He combined outdoor and indoor scenes and evolved the principle of film editing, of making a film by photographing and putting together separate shots, switching the audience's attention from the woman and child in the burning house to the ringing of the fire alarm and the dash of the fire engine to the house. Shots of events taking place simultaneously in different locations but with an important bearing on each other were used and created excitement and a new interest for the viewer. The basic elements of the film chase were evolved and were to be used repeatedly by directors for the next twenty years. It became clear that real time and film time need not coincide. Time could apparently stand still or go backwards while the camera showed what was happening in another area of action.

His second important film, *The Great Train Robbery* (1903), one of the first movie 'westerns', had fourteen different sequences. A group of bandits seeking to rob a train force a telegraph operator to deliver a false message and then leave him bound and gagged. They board the train, blow open the strong box, rob the passengers, and escape with the proceeds. The film switches back to the operator who calls for assistance by operating the telegraph key with his chin. Released by his daughter, he raises a posse from a western dance hall. They chase and kill the bandits in a wood and the film ends with a close-up of Barnes, the leader of the train robbers, firing a pistol point blank at the audience.

The film script was adapted from a stage melodrama of the same title by Scott Marble, produced at the Bowery Theatre in New York in 1896. But Porter told it in pictures with a style that was distinctively cinematic, enjoying a freedom and speed of movement which the theatre lacks. Shakespeare's plays, with their alternation of long and short scenes, incorporate a similar rhythm and movement, often accentuated by a rapid stage production. Some modern plays create even faster action by presenting simultaneous action in different sets on the same stage to give the effect of rapid cross-cutting. But this facility is available so much more readily to film directors, who can cut quickly from one scene to another and back again, or on to a third or fourth situation without waiting for a set to change or for fresh actors to appear. This mobility was first used by Porter, and later with supreme skill by Griffith and Eisenstein, to become a commonplace feature of the cinema. Later film directors, not satisfied with the flexibility which edited film can give, have attempted to imitate the stage technique of

building several different sets on one stage by using double
or multiple scenes on one screen picture. Abel Gance made use
of this idea in his triptych, or three-screen version, of *Napoléon*
in 1926.

Porter continued to make films for the Edison Company after
The Great Train Robbery. Even his ability to create excitement and
suspense on the screen must have been sorely tested by his commission in 1904 to make a 600-ft. film of *Parsifal*, Wagner's most
ponderous and static opera, which had a short time before
received its first American performance at the Metropolitan,
New York. He left Edison in 1909 to build up his own company,
Rex. This was only moderately successful and after a few years
he worked for Adolph Zukor's 'Famous Players' Company.
His last film, *The Eternal City*, was shot in Rome in 1915.
Although he lived on until 1941 he was dead as far as the
cinema was concerned after 1915. Méliès, Porter and D. W.
Griffith, whose career is discussed in the next chapter, three
of the greatest innovators in the early days of the cinema, all
dropped out of the industry before they were fifty-five. They
were not old physically, but in a medium which changed
rapidly in response to technical advances and the tastes of
predominantly young audiences, they were discarded by the
men who controlled the studios and decided what the public
wanted. Their fate contrasts sadly with that of some of the
great directors who emerged in the 1920s such as John Ford,
Jean Renoir and Alfred Hitchcock, who were still making films
forty years later.

Edwin Porter's longer narrative films were copied by other
companies. Better and more ambitious films deserved better
and more ambitious exhibition. Thomas Tally in Los Angeles
opened his 'Electric Theatre for up to date High Class Motion
Picture Entertainment Especially for Ladies and Children' in
1902. This was the first of many innovations from the city
destined to become the Californian centre of the world's film
industry. A year later George Hale, former chief of the Kansas
City Fire Department, showed films in a railroad carriage, with
a screen at one end on which travel films were projected while
the carriage rocked realistically from side to side rounding
imaginary curves and creating an illusion of movement. Hale's
Tours were a success and made two million dollars in two years,
but they perpetuated the novelty element of the cinema.

'*The Cascade Theatre*', *the Warner Brothers' first nickelodeon*

John P. Harris and Harry Davis opened their first 'nickelodeon' in Pittsburgh in 1905. The 'nickelodeon' introduced features destined to become characteristic of later, grander cinemas: cheap tickets (a nickel or 5 cents), an air of greater luxury than earlier converted shops and back rooms (though still primitive enough by the standards of the 1920s), continuous shows from 8 a.m. to midnight, and a piano accompaniment. Twelve months later there were over one hundred nickelodeons in Pittsburgh alone. Harris and Davis play no other great part in movie history, but their imitators included some of the great names of the industry – William Fox, Carl Laemmle (of Universal Films), Marcus Loew (later of Metro-Goldwyn-Mayer) and Adolph Zukor (the founder of the Paramount Company). Adolph Zukor celebrated his one hundredth birthday in January 1973 with a Paramount party in honour of a man whose association with motion pictures has ranged from *The Great Train Robbery* to *The Godfather*, almost the whole span of movie history. It is as though one man had been involved in the theatre from the days of *Gammer Gurton's Needle* to *Jesus Christ, Superstar*.

These men entered the motion picture business as the owners

or managers of nickelodeons. They ended up as the chairmen of companies making, distributing and exhibiting films throughout the world. They, like numerous other movie magnates, were Jews, first- or second-generation immigrants from Central or Eastern Europe. They worked hard and quickly saw the potential audience for films among their fellow immigrants who were crowding into the big manufacturing centres of America. Between 1900 and 1910 an average of nearly one million men, women and children settled in the United States every year. These newcomers spoke little or no English; other popular entertainments such as vaudeville shows were expensive and incomprehensible to many of them, but silent films could be enjoyed by all. Fox, Laemmle, Zukor, Loew, and fellow Polish, Russian or German Jews opened nickelodeons or ran distributing agencies to satisfy this audience. One physical characteristic common to nearly all the early film millionaires was their lack of height. Most of them were short men from generations of poorly fed, unhealthy ghetto families. Philip French in his book *The Movie Moguls* comments that 'One could have swung a scythe five and a half feet off the ground at a

The cinema as an extension of vaudeville: the Grand Pier at Weston-super-Mare, Somerset

A film poster advertises the visual attractions of a converted schoolroom, c. 1900

To-Night !   To-Night !

CALDER'S FAMOUS
CINEMATOGRAPH
AND
Popular Concert.

Don't miss seeing the Grand NEW PICTURES of

THE DREYFUS COURT MARTIAL.

The Prince of Wales in Edinburgh.
Sir Redvers Buller Embarking for Transvaal.
Scenes at the Highland Brigade Camp.
The Invercharron Gathering.
The Grand Fire Dance.
Barnum & Bailey's Procession.
The Mysterious Astrologer's Dream.
Spendid Train Scenes.
Grand Coloured Dances.
Comicalities and Burlesque Scenes, &c., &c.

Pictures of absorbing interest and Astounding Transformations.

SPLENDID • CONCERT
By First=Class Artistes.

DOORS OPEN AT 7.30.   CONCERT AT 8 P.M.
Popular Prices—See Bills.

A BRIGHT, UP TO DATE, SPARKLING ENTERTAINMENT.

The movies take their place alongside live entertainment

gathering of movie moguls without endangering many lives:
several would hardly have heard the swish.'[8]
The cinema-going habit also caught on in England. The Moss
Theatre group organized a cinema circuit; the Provincial
Cinematograph Group was formed in 1909, and by 1914
109 separate circuits were in existence. For the most part they
used converted shops, skating rinks (when the skating craze
died away), Mechanics Institutes and industrial buildings,
but Joshua Duckworth in 1907 commissioned the first custom-
built English picture house, the Central Hall in Colne. Ironically

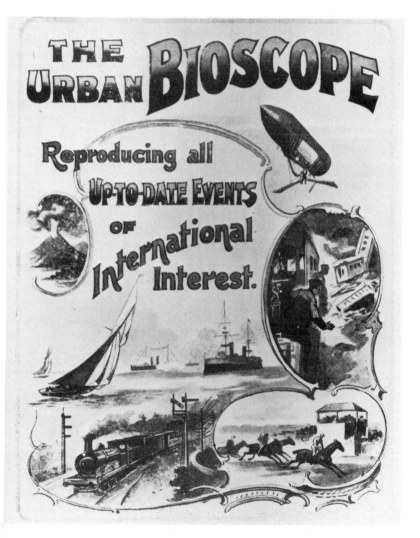

'Bioscope' brings the world to the people

it was later discarded as a cinema and used by an engineering firm.

But while America and Britain had the largest markets, France, following up the work of Lumière and Méliès, produced some of the best films and equipment. The strongest company was Pathé, with a French cockerel as its trade mark. By 1914 Pathé were manufacturing 80 per cent of the projectors in the world, and France was providing 60–70 per cent of the world's film exports. Their comedian, Max Linder, a precursor of Charlie Chaplin, to whom Chaplin later paid generous tribute, became one of the first world-famous stars, earning 200,000 francs a year.

Films were made in other countries including Denmark and Sweden. The Nordisk Danish company and the Svenska in Sweden established the foundations of a characteristically Scandinavian artistic film industry with a combination of slow, subtly photographed film stories and an element of eroticism largely absent from the other countries' products.

Just before the Great War the American industry had discovered Hollywood and the film star. Early American films

An early Biograph studio, in the days before movies went West

had been made in and around New York or Chicago. By 1918, for reasons outlined in Chapter 7, the majority of companies were established on the West Coast. Hollywood, a primitive township of four hundred inhabitants, was destined to dominate the world's movie industry and to be dominated by it. European production was concentrated in metropolitan centres: the French in Paris, German in Berlin and Munich, Russian in Moscow, British in and around London, Italian in Rome and Turin – small film studios in big cities. Hollywood contained big studios in a small town. That town was soon swallowed by Los Angeles, the biggest conurbation of all. But even then movies remained a major preoccupation of that city for over thirty years. By 1918 movies were Hollywood and by 1928 Hollywood was the movies.

The expansion in the number of cinemas increased the producers' profits. Films now told stories and created screen personalities. The actors and actresses who portrayed those personalities aroused the interest of the public, recognized the importance of that interest, and demanded a larger share of film receipts. Film stars were born and began to rival the fame and glamour of the great figures of the theatre and opera – Sarah Bernhardt, Sir Herbert Beerbohm Tree, Sir John Forbes-Robertson, Lily Langtry, Enrico Caruso, Galli Curci – and soon outstripped them in renown and income. Parts in the very earliest films had been played by the directors themselves and their families (Méliès featured in a vast number of his own films), by workpeople and by men and women drawn from the street. *The Workers Leaving the Lumière Factory of Lyons* were paid nothing for their appearance in the first film shown at the Grand Café. *Rescued by Rover*, made by Cecil Hepworth in 1905, was said to be the first British film for which the actors received payment. The early companies built up teams of men and women who acted, painted scenery, made costumes and swept the studio: they were operatives in a cottage industry. But with mass production and distribution came specialization.

Maurice Costello was one of the first to rebel: 'I am an actor and I will act, but I will not build sets and paint scenery.'[9] At first the managements were unwilling to publicize their actors, fearing a demand for higher status and higher salaries. But the public responded to the personalities that pleased them and wanted to know their names as they did those of stage actors or vaudeville entertainers. The answer one enquirer received from the Letter Column of the early film periodical *The Motion Picture Story Magazine* was: 'The "little lady" you mention is a Biograph player and there is a legend to the effect that Biograph players have their names locked in a big safe and only get them back when they leave the company.'[10] The legend may have been created by the editor of the magazine, which was itself published by the rival Vitagraph company, but it presupposes a desire to preserve anonymity. The public, however, remained curious about 'The Biograph Girl', Florence Lawrence, and her

A location shot for Uncle Tom's Cabin. *Specialization came later*

The young Charlie Chaplin photographed with Francis Xavier Bushman (left), one of the earliest screen heroes, and G. M. 'Broncho Billy' Anderson when all three were working for the Essanay Company

successor Mary Pickford. Their curiosity was satisfied and Mary Pickford soon became a highly paid film star. Mary dominated the film world from 1914 to 1924 in a way that no woman has ever dominated any other major industry. Mary as a business woman forcing male Company Presidents to accede to her salary demands anticipated the cry of the Women's Liberation Movement for equal status in the professional and commercial world, except that Mary sought a salary higher than and not equal to that of Charlie Chaplin. But the appeal that she exploited in support of her demands was the unashamedly feminine appeal of 'Little Mary' with her golden curls and sentimental charm. One of the few other women to achieve a comparable position in any other industry, Helena Rubenstein, built up her wealth and success by supplying cosmetics to help to attract the male.

The companies could not keep their actors and actresses anonymous forever. Stars' names were advertised and portrait posters appeared in cinema foyers. The fan mail began to flow in to the American studios at the same time as Max Linder was becoming a household name in France and Europe. Soon a Congressman's daughter returning from Sunday School confessed: 'Mamma, they asked us who we wanted to be like.' 'And?' queried her mother. 'Oh,' sighed the child, 'I told them the Lord, but I meant Mary Pickford.'[11]

Some of the most popular stars were the cowboys in the 'Westerns' which had already established themselves as a distinctive film form. The cinema could recount Western adventure stories far more effectively than the theatre and more vividly even than the books of Zane Grey. Many of the men who watched the films in which 'Broncho Billy' (G. M. Anderson), W. S. Hart and Tom Mix rode the range in the service of law

William S. Hart (the 'S' is for Shakespeare) temporarily abandons his horse

and order had themselves lived through the adventures of the pioneering West in the late 19th century. King Vidor, a Hollywood director in the 1920s and 1930s, recalls a visit to the cinema before 1914:

I once saw a West Texas cowboy draw his six-shooter and put several shots in the screen. He had come to town for a Saturday night's spree, but when he saw that the hero was about to be hung unjustly for cattle rustling he couldn't sit there with his six-shooter without doing something. The film did not stop, nor did they arrest the shooting cowboy. I suppose the three bullet holes were later patched, the manager having decided the less said about the incident the safer.[12]

These early cowboy films and the serial adventure stories like *Fantomas* from France or *Pearl White* from America provided an element of adventure and suspense for the growing urban cinema audiences throughout the world.

Such films were primitive compared with present-day cinemascope epics or sophisticated television dramas. They were hurriedly produced with very limited equipment. George Pearson's Pathé Studio of 1912 was, in his own words,

Pearl White, heroine of the serial The Perils of Pauline. *She later made films in Paris and died at Neuilly in 1938, a screen legend who had never worked in Hollywood*

a curious little place. The stage floor, some 20 ft. by 40 ft., was entirely lit by mercury vapour tubes: under the light everyone looked as though suffering from acute heart disease. All white apparel had to be tinted a violent primrose colour, and all pale complexions were similarly treated. The camera was mounted on a heavy capstan head bolted rigidly to the floor ... The camera angle was constant, dead on the centre of the set, with its two-inch lens equally permanent. A chalk line across the floor marked the down stage limit of the actors: if they dared move across it, their foot would be cut off in the camera view, an unforgiveable sin. I had a staff of five: cameraman, electrician, carpenter, scene painter and handyman.[13]

CHAPTER TWO
Movies develop style

Movies first appeared as brief records of everyday events, trains arriving, waves breaking, children eating, later of famous events, sporting, political, or social, and soon of simple stories told in pictures. Gradually they became more ambitious and complex. Méliès evolved a cinematic style of telling stories in a series of consecutive episodes and Porter heightened the drama by cross-reference from one incident to another. They appealed most to simple, even illiterate audiences, impressed by the mere novelty of movement on the screen. Films became longer as the technical limitations of photography and exhibition were overcome. With improved projectors, the pictures were brighter, less jerky and less of a strain on the eyes. Directors began to use sub-titles, fragments of dialogue or written narrative projected on to the screen between sequences to explain or expand the story. Descriptive titles were not very common before 1914 as their use slowed up the action, and many in the audience were unable to read them or could read only very slowly. The sub-titles of the silent cinema were shown as a separate sequence, usually before the action to which they referred. They rarely progressed to the sophistication of the sub-titles shown today with foreign-language films, where the translated dialogue is projected in white print at the foot of the moving film itself.

The cinema was searching for a style of its own. It was, as R. S. Randall has suggested, 'the first medium of communication without roots in either élite or folk culture'.[1] But it borrowed from the élite culture of the theatre by translating condensed stage classics on to the screen. In 1899 Sir Herbert Beerbohm Tree made a short film of *King John* featuring a scene not recorded by Shakespeare, the signing of the Magna Carta.

Shakespeare's limitations as a scenario writer were noted a few years later by the French director Zecca who, in adapting *Macbeth*, told a friend: 'I'm rewriting Shakespeare. The wretched fellow left out the most marvellous things.'[2] Sarah Bernhardt, the great French actress, at the age of fifty-six fought the duel scene in *Hamlet* for a three-minute film produced in 1900, and thereafter stories were frequently taken from Shakespeare and other classic dramatists and novelists.

As films lengthened – *Les Misérables* (1912) was 5000 metres long with five hours of film – companies began to seek to raise

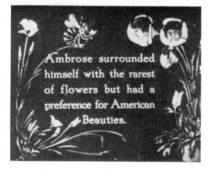
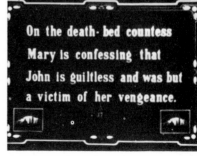

Descriptive sub-titles to illuminate the action

the quality and status of their product, both for prestige and because better films attracted a wealthier audience and commanded higher prices. The cinema was seeking to break out of the travelling booths and nickelodeons to become a superior entertainment. The earliest expressions of this urge came from France – deriving from, and in competition with, the wealth of theatre in Paris – and from Italy, with its origins in opera, a spectacle for the masses in the land of Verdi and Puccini. The Lafitte Brothers founded in 1907 the 'Film d'Art' Company in Paris and a year later produced the ambitious *Assassination of*

From France came the first stirrings of 'art'

the Duc de Guise performed by artists from the Comédie-Française. The scenario was written by the famous writer Lavedan and the musical accompaniment was composed for the occasion by Camille Saint-Saëns.

Music had become an important feature of film shows. At first it was played by a pianist or organist. Gradually trios and quartets were introduced and eventually the full symphony orchestras of the great picture palaces of the 1920s. Most of the musical scores were devised by the local performers. But some super-productions followed the lead set by *The Duc de Guise* and had recommended musical scores, either especially composed, as by Saint-Saëns or, later, by Honnegger for Abel Gance's *La Roue*, or, more frequently, made up from the appropriate sections of existing compositions. In 1924 the *Motion Picture Moods for Pianists and Organists, a Rapid Reference Collection of Selected Pieces Adapted to Fifty-Two Moods and Situations* was published. The recommended score for D. W. Griffith's *Judith of Bethulia* included excerpts from Rossini's *William Tell*, Suppé's *Poet and Peasant* Overture and Grieg's *Peer Gynt* Suite. The public was exposed to classical music which many of them, before the days of radio or the widespread availability of cheap gramophone records, heard for the first time in the movie houses. A reviewer of the Biograph film *A Fool's Revenge*, based on Verdi's *Rigoletto*, wrote in the *Motion Picture World* in 1909 that 'a pleasant variation from the eternal ragtime was a refined deliverance of classical music, corresponding to the character of the picture, including Schumann's *Träumerei* and Beethoven's *Moonlight Sonata*. The first time, indeed, we have ever heard Beethoven in a five-cent theatre.'[3] No attempt seems to have been made to link Biograph's *A Fool's Revenge* with Verdi's music. Cinemas provided employment for thousands of musicians. Many famous performers started their professional careers in the orchestra pit of their local picture palace.

Not only performers but even composers depended on the cinema. Shostakovich, the Soviet composer, earned his living in this way in the starvation years of 1924–5, as his wife described in a letter.

Mitya is going to work in a movie house. This is a real tragedy for us, considering the hard work and his health. But he says that he cannot stand our life any longer and will feel much better if he could bring home some money every month . . . Down in front of the screen sat Mitya, his back soaked with perspiration, his near-sighted eyes in their horn-rimmed glasses peering upwards to follow the story, his fingers pounding away on the raucous upright-piano. Late at night he trudged home in a thin coat and summer cap, with no warm gloves or galoshes, and arrived exhausted around one o'clock in the morning ... It was in the midst of this that Mitya began composing his First Symphony.[4]

Musical accompaniments had originally been produced to drown the noise of the early projectors. The cafés and music halls in which most early shows were given already employed musicians for their other entertainments. Soon other more dramatic sound effects were introduced: pistol shots, train bells, the roll of thunder. Even after projectors were separately housed and could no longer be so clearly heard, music was retained to drown the noise of the audience coughing, spitting or reading the sub-titles aloud. It soon became an integral part of the film itself, being used to suggest emotion or tragedy, to increase suspense or stimulate excitement. Twenty years later, in 1928, a musical background was so much an accepted feature of the entertainment that Ernest Betts in his book *Heraclitus: The Future of Films* could applaud a move to show completely silent films. 'I think it was the London Film Society which first gave the public an opportunity of seeing silent drama that was really silent when they showed *Roskolnikov* without music in their 1926 season. I do not know how far that experiment was a success, but it is something that it was an experiment, that it broke free from custom, introduced a new idea and left the eye free to take in the story by itself.'[5] The experiment was not often repeated. Within a short time the sound track appeared, bringing a range of musical backgrounds and musical clichés that no pit pianist or orchestra could rival. But music, even of the most elementary variety, was an essential part of the early film experience, and it is a pity that silent film presentations to clubs and societies at the present time are all too often given without an orchestral or even a piano accompaniment. Silent films seen today without musical backing are an incomplete experience. Ivor Montagu in his *Film World* asserts: 'To see a "silent" film cold and silent is like attending a play-reading, better said, much worse, like attending the reading of the libretto

Music for emotion: filming with the aid of a violin

of an opera. It requires an effort of imagination and resources of professional experience to be able to conceive even a shadow of what the real thing might be like.'[6]

Actors as well as audiences needed music. Directors used it on the set and many players demanded it to put them in the right mood for a dramatic scene. The English director Adrian Brunel worked on *Woman to Woman*, made in 1923 with the American star Betty Compson. He records that although (perhaps because) she was an experienced film actress, 'she was incapable of registering emotion without the aid of a three-piece orchestra (piano, cello, violin). Throughout most of the scenes in *Woman to Woman* this orchestra would churn out *Mighty Like a Rose* and Miss Compson would then perform and cry real tears (glycerine not being required): to this day I cannot hear *Mighty Like a Rose* without wanting to burst a blood vessel.'[7]

The Assassination of the Duc de Guise was followed by a series of other superior films by Gaumont and Pathé Companies as well as by 'Film d'Art'. Scenarios were commissioned from great writers like Edmond Rostand, Sardou, Jules Lemaître and Anatole France. Sarah Bernhardt, Albert Réjane and Coquelin performed in them. Like most great figures drawn from the stage into the film studio, they were unconvincing and succeeded only by virtue of their stage reputation. Deprived of their voices and a chance to declaim, their actions seemed exaggerated and laughable even to early cinema audiences. When Sir Herbert Beerbohm Tree acted a film version of *Macbeth* in Hollywood he insisted on delivering all the speeches in full, even though the film was silent. This involved a substantial waste of film since the silent movie sequence needed only a fraction of the time involved in speaking all the lines. After a few days the director instructed the cameraman to photograph the amount of film necessary for each scene and then to disengage the camera mechanism, so that the handle was turned, to satisfy Sir Herbert's vanity, but no film was exposed. The finished article with sub-titles composed by Anita Loos, later to write the best-selling novel *Gentlemen Prefer Blondes,* was a commercial and artistic failure. It was not enough to photograph a successful stage performance and imagine that this would make a satisfactory film. Forbes-Robertson, Caruso, Pavlova and other stars of the theatre, opera and ballet failed to master the new medium. John Barrymore in America, Godfrey Tearle in England, Maurice Chevalier in France were some of the few who were able to move successfully from the theatre to the cinema, and even they became more effective after the arrival of the talkies. A more naturalistic style of acting was developed by the dramatic stars of the cinema like Richard Barthelmess, Lillian Gish, Werner Krauss or Sessue Hayakawa.

Richard Barthelmess appeared in his first film in 1913 and became a major star six years later with his role as the Chinese hero of *Broken Blossoms* with Lillian Gish. Twenty years later he was still in Hollywood acting in *Only Angels Have Wings* with Rita Hayworth. Lillian Gish's career has lasted even longer, from the early D. W. Griffith pre-1914 Biograph films, through *The Birth of a Nation, Intolerance* and *Broken Blossoms* into the sound era and the television drama of the 1960s. She has also acted in many stage plays in America and Britain. In 1936 she was Ophelia to John Gielgud's *Hamlet* on Broadway. Werner Krauss was one of the many capable actors to appear in the German films of the 1920s. He played the role of Caligari in the most famous of all German productions and unlike many of his contemporaries stayed in Europe even after the decline

D. W. Griffith's ideal of feminine beauty, Lillian Gish

Werner Krauss, a leading German actor from Caligari to Hitler

Sessue Hayakawa, impressing as a golfer

of the German industry; he appeared in the films of the Nazi period, most notably the anti-semitic *Jew Süss* produced in 1940. Sessue Hayakawa acted effectively in films produced in his native Japan, and also in America and France from 1909 to *The Bridge on the River Kwai* in 1957. Although all four had received their early training in the pre-war theatre, they were not established stage actors and actresses when they began to make films. They created an acting style specifically designed to convey emotions without words, by the use of gestures and of the eyes and hands, which could be recorded by the camera in close-up shots and still be clearly seen by the audience at the back of the cinema. A film actor is scrutinized by millions of people more closely than any stage actor is even by the fortunate few at the front of the stalls.

Other film stars succeeded by virtue of their personality rather than their acting skill, like Mary Pickford, Gloria Swanson, Rudolph Valentino or Ramon Novarro. Their appeal lay in who they were rather than in their ability to portray a variety of characters. Experience in the legitimate theatre could for some be an insurmountable handicap. Even later, in the sound studio

The Flying Fleet *(1929) was one of many films shot as a silent but given a musical sound-track after completion. Ramon Novarro, the star of the film, is seen with the composer Percy Grainger*

Gloria Swanson, one of the Keystone bathing beauties, in the grip of Mack Swain (1916)

of the 1950s, Frederic March, equally distinguished in both media, apologized to his director: 'Sorry I did it again. I keep forgetting – this is a movie and I mustn't act.'[8] He at least was aware of the pitfall: many earlier stage recruits to the cinema were unconscious of it. They brought from the theatre of the pre-1914 era a high-flown declamatory style of performance, which the cinema eventually helped to drive off the stage itself.

Sarah Bernhardt's *Queen Elizabeth*, made in England in 1912, was not a convincing film but its grandeur and the fame of the greatest living actress made it a commercial success throughout Europe and in the United States. Adolph Zukor bought the American distribution rights for 20,000 dollars and made a handsome profit by showing it in the theatres as an art film and charging theatre-seat prices. Inspired by this coup he formed the 'Famous Players Company' to distribute, and even to make, more such ambitious films. Others followed him including 'The Jesse Lasky Feature Play Company' linking Lasky with Cecil B. DeMille and Samuel Goldfish (later to take the name Samuel Goldwyn). Zukor and Lasky had little success with 'famous plays and famous players' but produced many other less pretentious films, later merging into the 'Paramount Company', the major force in Hollywood in the 1920s.

American directors were more impressed by the great Italian crowd spectaculars, which introduced a new style into the cinema and established a tradition which continued with D. W. Griffith's *Intolerance*, Niblo's *Ben Hur*, Cecil B. DeMille's *King of Kings* and *The Ten Commandments*, through to the mammoth Cinemascope productions of the 1950s and 1960s, *El Cid*, *Cleopatra*, *Spartacus*, and *The Bible*. In 1908 the first outstanding Italian movie appeared, *The Last Days of Pompeii*. A second version was produced in 1913, followed by *Quo Vadis* which cost £6940 to make and brought in £70,000. A play called *Quo Vadis* had been produced on the New York stage, and Hilary Bell, *New York Herald* critic, had commented: 'In the play we see several horses galloping on a moving platform. They make no headway and the moving scenery behind them does not delude the spectators into the belief that they are racing...The only way to secure the exact sense of action for this incident in a theatre is to represent it by Mr Edison's invention.'[9] The Italians filmed the whole story, including a

One of the giant sets used for Cabiria *(1914), an epic film about the Punic Wars in Ancient Rome, a theme made popular by the Italian conquest of Libya in 1911*

A chariot race from a late Italian spectacular, Messalina *(1924)*

chariot race, repeated in the later famous contests in the American silent and sound versions of *Ben Hur*. *Quo Vadis* lasted for over two hours and was shown in a Broadway theatre with seats costing up to $1·50 instead of the usual 15 cents in the cinema. In London it was screened in the Albert Hall. *Cabiria*, most famous of the pre-war Italian films, was made from a script attributed to Gabriele d'Annunzio, well-known Italian writer and flamboyant precursor of Mussolini, but written in fact by the director Pastrone. Part of its expenses was covered by American financial backers. This was an early example of the American financial domination of the world cinema and anticipated the contemporary large-scale European productions spawned by Hollywood companies. Such films took the camera out of the confines of the studio and away from the limited costs of most earlier productions, and showed how to capitalize on the ability of the cinema to marshal crowds far larger than those to be found in even the most lavish Italian opera houses. The crowd scenes of operas such as *Aïda* and *Don Carlos* had suggested a new dimension for the motion picture that was later developed by Hollywood producers and shown to mid-Western audiences to whom Verdi was unknown.

These two developments of cinema as an art form (French filmed stage plays and Italian spectaculars) were both derived from existing traditions and techniques. They were only the translation and extension of theatrical or operatic styles for the camera. Even Vitagraph's 1912 *Indian Romeo and Juliet*, with Florence Turner and Wallace Reid playing the leads as the star-crossed lovers of the Huron and Mohican tribes, was only a regional variation on an established theme. However, the early American comedies of John Bunny and Flora Finch, and of Mack Sennett for the Keystone Company, together with the output of Max Linder in France and Charlie Chaplin in Hollywood, were creating a specifically cinematic technique and art, derived from the miming and comic routines of the French and English music halls or American vaudeville shows. (Buster Keaton was still touring the American vaudeville circuit with his parents as he had done from the age of six.) At the same time the greatest creative director in the American silent cinema, D. W. Griffith, was evolving his own style of film-making in a series of short and medium-length films that were to lead to his masterpiece *The Birth of a Nation*.

James Agee has summarized Griffith's achievement:

As a director Griffith hit the picture business like a tornado. Before he walked on the set motion pictures had been, in actuality, static. At a respectful distance the camera snapped a series of whole scenes clustered in the groupings of a stage play. Griffith broke up the pose. He rammed his camera into the middle of the action. He took close-ups, cross-cuts, angle shots and dissolves. His camera was alive picking off shots; then he built the shots into sequences, the sequences into tense, swift narrative. For the first time the movies had a man who realized that while a theatre audience listened, a movie audience watched.[10]

Griffith himself said: 'Above all...I am trying to make you see.'

The son of a colonel in the Confederate Army, Griffith carried with him throughout his life many of the graces and prejudices and much of the generosity of the American South. Early experience as a journalist, fireman, wandering poet, metal worker and stage actor gave him a background he later drew on for characters and incidents in his films. He came to New York in 1906 as an actor and joined Thomas Dixon's theatrical company which had just finished a tour with *The Clansman*.

David Wark Griffith and friend

The baby was later 'rescued from an eagle's nest' by Griffith, whose experience in this film confirmed his initial contempt for the cinema

(Eight years later Griffith was to use the play as the basis for *The Birth of a Nation*.) His main ambition at that time was to become a playwright. His first play, *The Fool and the Girl*, closed after a few performances in Washington. Griffith then worked in New York on another play, *War*, dramatizing incidents in the American War of Independence. In a desperate attempt to earn money he offered a story based on Puccini's opera *Tosca* to the Edison Film Company. He was received by Edwin S. Porter, who did not want the script but instead hired him as an actor for *Rescued from an Eagle's Nest*. Griffith played the hero, a woodcutter who saves a baby stolen by an eagle. Griffith finished the film in one day and left with his stage contempt for the new entertainment undiminished. But the theatre was equally unimpressed by his talents and Griffith was back in 1908 in the studio of the American Mutoscope and Biograph Company. He became a film director, his first production, *The Adventures of Dollie*, being released on 14 July 1908. In the following six years he turned out nearly four hundred short films. This experience taught him the possibilities and limitations of the camera. He formed a close understanding with his cameraman, Billy Bitzer, who was responsible for much of the graphic beauty of their later films. Griffith found and encouraged other talents, bringing into the studios Michael Sinott (Mack Sennett), Mary Pickford, Mae Marsh, Dorothy and Lillian Gish, Mabel Normand, Lionel Barrymore and many other later stars. He moved the camera close to and far away from his actors and built up his stories from fragments by switching the camera from one character or episode to another. He no longer photographed action from one standard distance against a flat theatrical set, relying on a series of stage-play sequences to convey narrative effect and character interest. Edwin Porter had pioneered this approach and was still making films, but Griffith brought to the cinema a new touch of genius and creative imagination.

His ideas were not automatically understood and appreciated. His wife Linda Arvidson recalls a controversy aroused by his plans for *After Many Years*, a movie based on Tennyson's poem *Enoch Arden* (Griffith had a great feeling for the sentimentalism and melodrama of many Victorian poems and plays).

When Mr Griffith suggested a scene showing Annie Lee waiting for her husband's return to be followed by a scene showing Enoch cast away on a desert island, it was altogether too distracting.
    'How can you tell a story jumping about like that? The people won't know what it's about.'
    'Well,' said Mr Griffith, 'doesn't Dickens write that way?'
    'Yes, but that's Dickens' novel writing; that's different.'
    'Oh not so much, these are picture stories; not so different.'[11]

Griffith in an interview published in 1917 emphasized that he 'borrowed the "cut back" from Charles Dickens. Novelists think nothing of leaving one set of characters in the midst of affairs and going back to deal with earlier events in which another set of characters is involved.'[12]

Griffith brought many other elements of the novel to the cinema: characterization, descriptions of the settings within which his characters lived and worked, rapid alternating narrative, a succession of incidents to create interest and tension. But the novels that Griffith understood and copied were the formal narrative novels of the 19th century, those of Dickens and Thackeray, not the more sensitive, subtle works of Proust, Kafka, James Joyce, that were being written at the time. He was probably unaware that these existed and there is no evidence that he ever read them. He was not a traditionally cultured man like the Russian director Eisenstein whose written work on the cinema refers to authors as varied as Shakespeare, Kafka, Flaubert, Joyce, Lévy-Bruhl and Dreiser. Griffith and Eisenstein both died in 1948 having lost favour with the film industry they helped to create, one for personal and artistic reasons, the other for political ones. But their combined achievements were more important than those of any other two directors. Jay Leyda has written: 'The anti-intellectualism of the one and the super-intellectualism of the other together formed the background of film art in its first fifty years of life.'[13] Eisenstein and other Russian, German and French directors understood and appreciated the intellectual ideas of their day and tried to incorporate some of them into their work. Eisenstein's *October*, Wiene's *The Cabinet of Dr Caligari*, Abel Gance's *La Roue* appeal to (and to some extent can only be fully appreciated by) an intellectual taste beyond that of the average cinema-goer. Hollywood employed few intellectuals except for some imported European directors and writers hired to produce scripts. But amidst their mass of indifferent movies they produced some films of outstanding visual beauty and dramatic quality which rank among the masterpieces of the cinema. Griffith, Thomas Ince, Charlie Chaplin, Buster Keaton, John Ford were not conventionally educated men, but they created great films that were artistic achievements of a new kind.

Griffith used no clearly formulated script. He carried a general outline of the story in his head and devised cinematic ways of telling it as he went along. It was an expensive, haphazard style of creation and it could only work as long as filming costs were comparatively low and his stock of original ideas lasted out. But the grandiose, disorganized manner in which he made *Intolerance*, his mammoth study in prejudice in four ages filmed in 1916, exhausted all the profits from *The Birth of a Nation* and restricted his subsequent filming possibilities.

Early on Griffith had acquired a reputation for extravagance in an industry that was still thinking in terms of one-reel (twelve-minute) films made for a few hundred dollars. In 1913, aroused by the scale of the imported Italian films, he produced his own biblical film *Judith of Bethulia* in four reels. The Biograph Company protested and said that in future he would only be

A poster advertises Civilization, *Thomas Ince's plea for pacifism made in 1916*

allowed to supervise production and not to direct. Griffith moved to the Reliance-Majestic Studios (the second half of the name was at least appropriate), made four short films for them, and then launched into a film version of *The Clansman,* the Reverend Thomas Dixon's play dealing with the aftermath of he Civil War in the American South and telling a story of Southern chivalry and Yankee political corruption. A critic called the stage production 'as crude a melodrama as ever slipped its anchor and drifted westwards from 3rd Avenue'.[14] The film also was melodramatic but made great cinema.

The Birth of a Nation opens with an historical prologue showing Negroes being sold as slaves and asserting that 'The bringing of the African to America planted the first seeds of disunion'. Attention is then switched to the two families, the Stonemans representing the North and the Camerons the South. The Stonemans are visiting the Southern family and the sons and daughters become close friends. The title, 'Chums – The Younger Sons: North and South', suggests a relationship soon to be broken by war, which is shown in the film by shots of President Lincoln in Washington and scenes of a battle in which Tod Stoneman falls dead on the body of Wade Cameron. After the war Ben Cameron is in hospital in Washington tended by Elsie Stoneman but under sentence of death. He is, however, pardoned by Lincoln and returns home to the South, where the climax of the film begins.

Griffith portrays 'Reconstruction' as a Southerner sees it. The defeated Confederate States are exploited by unscrupulous Yankee politicians from the North. The liberated Negro slaves are encouraged to reject and torment their former masters and friends. The head of the Stoneman family, himself a Northern politician, encourages his half-caste protégé, Silas Lynch, who becomes Lieutenant-Governor. A Negro servant, Gus, who has joined Lynch's militia, attempts to rape Flora Cameron. She escapes through the woods and hurls herself over a cliff, carrying her honour through 'the opal gates of death' as the title explains. The plot becomes more complex. Ben Cameron becomes an active member of the Ku Klux Klan and is helped by Phil Stoneman from the North. Together they are besieged by Negroes in a small cabin. 'The former enemies of North and South are united again in common defence of their Aryan birthright.' Lynch wants to marry Elsie Stoneman and holds

Elsie and her father in his head-quarters. Finally the Ku Klux
Klansmen rescue all the besieged Camerons and Stonemans.
The two young couples, Margaret and Phil and Elsie and Ben,
marry and unite the two families and the two halves of a divided
nation. The last title declares: 'Liberty and Union, one and
inseparable, now and forever.'

Thomas Dixon sold the screen rights of his play for 2500
dollars and 25 per cent of the profits. The film itself cost 100,000
dollars to make and was completed in nine weeks. It has since
been shown all over the world and is still in demand as a major
achievement in the history of the cinema. Robert Henderson
estimates that its total box office takings amount to over $48
million. The film was first shown as *The Clansman* in California
in January 1915 but when it opened in New York on 3 March at
the Liberty Theatre with a 40-piece orchestra and a chorus, its
title had been changed to *The Birth of a Nation*. It ran for forty-
four weeks, created a political sensation, and was shown to
enthusiastic audiences all over America.

Nevertheless, many voices were raised against the film and its
glorification of the Ku Klux Klan. Griffith had cut out some of
the most inflammatory sequences denouncing the hypocrisy of
the New England abolitionists, whom he portrayed as being
descendants of slave traders; he also omitted the reference to a
letter from Lincoln to his Secretary of War Stanton suggesting
that Negroes were inferior to white men. The National Association for the Advancement of Coloured People attacked the film
and was supported by the President of Harvard University and
many leading writers and politicians. A private showing
was given for Woodrow Wilson in Washington. His secretary
had to fend off the criticism which this aroused by explaining:
'I beg to say that it is true that *The Birth of a Nation* was produced
before the President and his family at the White House, but the
President was entirely unaware of the character of the play
before it was presented and has at no time expressed his appro-
bation of it. Its exhibition at the White House was a courtesy
extended to an old acquaintance.'[15]

The film was brought to the notice of the United States
Senate. The possibility of official action prompted Thomas
Dixon to send this cable to James E. Martine, the Democratic
Senator for New Jersey:

Censorship of motion pictures is the most dangerous attack on

American liberty since the foundation of the Republic … Our fathers fled the Old World to escape this and founded the Republic to free the human mind from shackles. Shall we go back to the Dark Ages? I first preached *The Clansman* as a sermon. No censor dared to silence my pulpit. I turned my sermon into a lecture and delivered it from Miami to California without license. I turned the lecture into a novel and no censor has yet stopped the press of Doubleday Page and Company. I turned the novel into a spoken play and no censor has dared to interfere. I turned the play into a motion picture and it has cost me seventy-five thousand dollars in lawyers' fees to fight the censors the first ten months. This condition of affairs is infamous. It is the immediate duty of Congress to reaffirm the principle of free speech in America and abolish all censors.[16]

Privately he was delighted by the controversy. 'The silly legal opposition they are giving will make me a millionaire if they keep it up.'[17] Griffith was more concerned and in 1916 wrote a pamphlet *The Rise and Fall of Free Speech in America* in which he argued that 'The motion picture is a medium of expression as clean and decent as any mankind has ever discovered. A people that would allow the suppression of this form of speech would unquestionably submit to the suppression of that which we all consider so highly, the printing press.'[18]

The allegations that he had shown racial intolerance prompted Griffith to plan an even more ambitious film, featuring intolerance on a grand scale and making clear his own hatred of religious and social discrimination. His vast, at times incoherent, film *Intolerance* was based on four stories of persecution – of Christ himself, of the fall of Babylon, of the Huguenots in 16th-century France, and of a modern industrial working family. It cost twenty times as much to make as *The Birth of a Nation*, took over a year to complete during which seventy-six hours of material were shot, and staggered Hollywood by the scale of its sets and the size of its cast. The sets and crowd scenes are overwhelming even when one sees it today and realizes that the walls of Babylon and Belshazzar's palace are full-size constructions and not models photographed and 'blown up'. The cast included many of the great names of the early Hollywood era – Lillian Gish, Constance Talmadge, Wallace Reid, Eugene Pallette, Joseph Henaberry, Bessie Love, Erich von Stroheim, Mae Marsh, Robert Harron, Monte Blue, and lost in the crowd scenes are many guest stars such as Douglas Fairbanks,

Sir Herbert Beerbohm Tree, Carole Dempster. Eventually the film was cut to three hours and opened in New York in September 1916. Audiences were curious, were impressed, but the film was never to be considered artistically satisfying. It ends with not one but three of the suspense-chase scenes so beloved by Griffith and by all early film-makers. The Mountain Girl races back to warn Babylon of the return of the Persian army, the Huguenot hero Eugene Latour tries to save his fiancée from the massacre of St Bartholomew, and the heroine in the modern story *The Dear One* pursues the State Governor's train to convince him of the innocence of her husband and then dashes to the gaol to save him from the hangman's noose. *Intolerance* was much admired by the later Russian directors who used crowds and great emotional themes much more dynamically.

After *Intolerance* Griffith made many more films – *Broken Blossoms* (1919), *Way Down East* (1920), *Orphans of the Storm* (1922) – of great charm and skill, but his major contribution to the art of the cinema had already been made with his early Biograph films and his two great epics. He lived in Hollywood for seventeen years after his last production *The Struggle* (1931),

One of Griffith's last films was a remake in 1928 of The Battle of the Sexes *with Sally O'Neil, Billy Bennett and William Bakewell. Shot as a silent the film had one song and a musical sound-track added later*

a disappointed and disappointing man. He had, however, done more than enough to ensure himself a place of supreme importance in the history of the cinema and of 20th-century culture.

An equally important place is occupied by Charlie Chaplin. Chaplin entered the movies only a few years after Griffith but was still producing and directing films thirty-five years after Griffith's last major production. Chaplin and his associates and rivals did for screen comedy what Griffith had done for drama.

Although all his best work was carried out in America, Chaplin was born in England on 16 April 1889, four days before Hitler. As a child he was poor and hungry. His experiences in crowded, wretched Victorian London gave him a bitter understanding of human behaviour, softened by a sentimentalism very similar to that of Griffith himself. Had they been filming seventy years earlier both of them would have found it easy to use scripts written by Dickens. Chaplin followed his parents on to the stage and became a member of Fred Karno's music-hall troupe. Here he had learned the art of mime and comedy timing: he watched acrobats, jugglers and comedians working to 'hold' an audience. Techniques and experience absorbed in

Charlie Chaplin (centre) with the Fred Karno troupe, including Stan Laurel on left, en route for his first visit to America in 1910

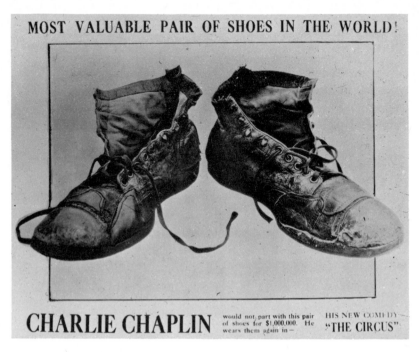

MOST VALUABLE PAIR OF SHOES IN THE WORLD!

CHARLIE CHAPLIN would not part with this pair of shoes for $1,000,000. He wears them again in — HIS NEW COMEDY — "THE CIRCUS"

Part of the tramp's equipment

England were soon to be combined with the speed and flexibility provided by Hollywood cameramen and studio crews to create some of the funniest films ever made.

Chaplin had toured America with the Karno Company in 1910. He returned in 1912. The following year he was invited into the studios by Mack Sennett, who had left D. W. Griffith to make slapstick comedies for the Keystone Company. After a tentative beginning Chaplin hit on the tramp costume – bowler hat, moustache, baggy trousers, outsize boots, and cane. With it he took on the personality of the tramp, always trying to make good in conventional society but almost always thwarted by bad luck or his own inadequacy. This plight was understood by millions in his audience, the men and women of industrial cities living in the midst of a wealth and comfort they could never enjoy but remaining hopeful that a better day was coming. Charlie's disasters were their disasters, and his victories, usually over enemies bigger or richer than the tramp, were their victories. Chaplin outlined the character of his hero as 'many-sided, a tramp, a gentleman, a poet, a dreamer, a lonely fellow, always hopeful of romance and adventure. He would have you believe he is a scientist, a musician, a duke, a polo-player. However, he is not above picking up a cigarette butt or robbing a baby of its candy.'[19]

Once he had mastered his new role Charlie starred in a succession of short films that carried the tramp all over the world and brought Chaplin the success denied to his screen character. He moved from company to company at vastly increased salaries until he had enough money to produce, direct, write, appear in and finance his own full-length films. These were distributed by United Artists, the millionaires' film co-operative of Chaplin, Pickford, Fairbanks and Griffith. Chaplin achieved universal popularity with all classes in all countries, entertaining mass audiences and winning the respect of statesmen and intellectuals who earnestly analysed the reasons for his unparalleled success. His early shorts *The Pawnshop* (1916) and *Easy Street* (1917), his middle period medium-length films *Shoulder Arms* (1918) and *The Kid* (1921), and his major independent productions *The Gold Rush* (1925) and *City Lights* (1931) showed developments in characterization but few technical improvements. The formula, however, satisfied his public.

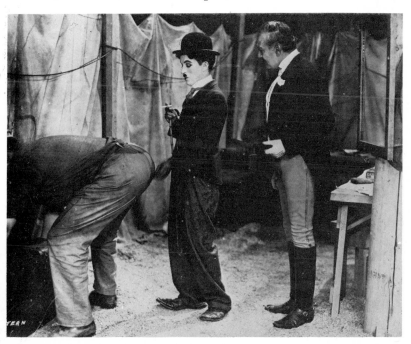

Chaplin in The Circus *(1928), his last silent film. Although* City Lights *(1930) was not a talkie it had a sound-track of music composed by Chaplin*

Three ages of Buster Keaton, as a baby, as a stage character and travelling trouper with his parents, and finally (below) as a proud father

Chaplin was only one film comedian, though perhaps the greatest, to serve his apprenticeship in the Keystone studios. Others included 'Fatty' Arbuckle, Ford Sterling, Louise Fazenda, Chester Conklin, Slim Summerville, Mack Swain and Carole Lombard. Sennett created two groups of performers – the Keystone Cops and the Mack Sennett bathing beauties – and the film pantomime of the custard pie and the comedy of violent chases. His inventiveness was rivalled in the 1920s by the output of the Hal Roach Studios, a producing company in Culver City specializing in comedies which encouraged the talent of Harold Lloyd and Laurel and Hardy.

Other great figures from the world of crazy comedy and mimed humour were Buster Keaton and Harry Langdon. David Robinson has written: 'Keaton and Chaplin have in common that everything they do seems new and spontaneous; their comedy seems to be snatched from life as it passes, the response of an original vision.'[20] Keaton's films of the 1920s, such as *The General*, *Sherlock Jr* and *The Navigator*, are the silent comedies most highly praised by the critics of today. His reputation has soared while that of Chaplin has declined. Keaton's philosophy

One of Mack Sennett's most famous comedians, Chester Conklin. Conklin came from Barnum's circus into Chaplin's first film, Making a Living *(1914)*

DRESSING
ROOM

CHARLIE CHAPLIN
BETTY COMPSON
FORD STERLING
EVELYN PUN
CHAP MURRAY
BEBE DANIELS
HAROLD LLOYD
GLORIA SWANSON
HARRY LANGDON

The comedian with the baby face – Harry Langdon

of bewildered contempt for his innumerable enemies and his stoic acceptance of misfortune command more favour than the 'busyness' of Chaplin. Charlie worked hard for his laughs and now that his tricks are well known the laughs are harder to come by. But although Keaton is now more highly regarded there is no doubt that fifty years ago Chaplin was more universally popular and is more significant in the history of the cinema.

The styles of Harry Langdon and Harold Lloyd were very different from each other. Langdon was even weaker and more easily put upon than Keaton. His sad, white face made him look, as James Agee commented, like an elderly baby, and he wandered like an overgrown baby through life. Harold Lloyd, although sometimes discomfited, was potentially like many other successful young Americans in the 1920s, with his casual clothes, horn-rimmed glasses, breezy college-boy personality, and his life amidst crowded streets and skyscrapers. Chaplin, Keaton and Langdon were more timeless and universal in their characterization and each had an element of melancholy in their film character. Perhaps it is not surprising that Harold Lloyd was the only one to enjoy a successful and uncomplicated

Harold Lloyd in Safety Last *before the climb which ended on the hands of an outsize clock*

Harold Lloyd in a tight spot

Although Buster Keaton never played a romantic hero his profile was as striking as that of any leading man (The General, *1926*)

personal and business life. When he retired he was one of the richest men in Hollywood.

These are only four of the many great comedians of the American silent cinema. From the other film-producing countries only Max Linder can claim equal fame. In the contemporary cinema there are no comedians producing a regular output of successful features. Even one genuinely funny film is a rare event. Yet from 1913 to 1928 almost every cinema in the Western world included a comedy in every programme, even if it was only a one-reel short, and almost all of these were American.

Max Linder (centre right) in a pre-1914 French comedy. Bottom left is the cockerel, the Pathé trade mark

The skills of cameramen, set designers, stunt men and actors were harnessed by the fertile imagination of the 'gag men' who invented more and more outrageously absurd plots and situations.

Hollywood comedies did more than any other type of film to establish American screen supremacy. France produced no successor to Max Linder, who solved the problem of translating stage humour into the film studio and showed how to produce laughs without words. These silent film comedies, and early Chaplin shorts in particular, have been debased by overexposure in television programmes, which sometimes snatch extracts from complete films and show them at the wrong speeds with vulgar sound tracks grafted on to them. This ill-treatment should not be allowed to disguise their true value and their importance as an essential element in the development of motion picture technique.

CHAPTER THREE

Movies become an art form

During the First World War, American movies (above all, those of Griffith and Cecil B. DeMille) had pioneered technical and artistic developments. European production was severely restricted owing to the wartime calls on men and materials. Not even an international star like Max Linder was excused from military service. Celluloid was used for explosives as well as for films. The Allied blockade split the European market and the Central Powers had to be content with German and Scandinavian films. French and Italian output fell catastrophically. The British cinema had never attained high standards after the promise of its first decade (1895–1905). America seized the opportunity to fill this gap and produced the most exciting new movies. Her commercial supremacy, at least, was never subsequently challenged, even though European studios produced most of the outstanding artistic achievements of the 1920s.

After the Versailles Peace Conference the European nations began to rebuild their film industries. Trade and cultural links between the belligerent nations were re-established, but for several years films from Germany were not welcomed in the cinemas of her recent enemies. The official British ban on German film imports was dropped in 1920 but the Exhibitors' Association was still discussing in December 1921 whether it should continue the ten-year embargo it had decided upon in 1918. Although this was abandoned in the following year the immediate post-war German films, including *The Cabinet of Dr Caligari,* were not shown publicly in London until 1923. The silent films from Soviet Russia were never widely known despite their technical brilliance. Nevertheless both Germany and the U.S.S.R. surmounted these handicaps and produced some of the greatest advances in the cinematic art. For a short period interesting films were made in Sweden and Denmark but all too soon they lost their best stars and directors to Germany and America. Italian production slumped both in quantity and quality, and intermittent British attempts to raise the artistic standards of its small-scale and theatrically dominated industry failed.

Germany's skilled electrical and optical industries helped to equip some of the best studios in Europe. A former Zeppelin airship hangar, emptied by the treaty restrictions on German aviation, was converted by the Staaken Film Company into a studio that could be used by eight teams simultaneously. From these studios emerged a succession of imaginative films, tortured and introspective, very different from Griffith's epics or sentimental dramas, and much less happy and self-confident than the comedies or romances of Hollywood. They were typical of Weimar Germany, which was struggling to create a new society out of the ruins of a defeated militaristic and authoritarian state, torn by the conflict between democratic and revengeful nationalist political movements, but alive with the artistic excitement of Germany in the 1920s – the home of Expressionist art, the Bauhaus movement in architecture, and the music of Schönberg and Kurt Weill.

Before 1914 Germany had produced few films of note, despite its strong theatrical tradition. Max Reinhardt, a leading figure in European dramatic production, had directed films; Hugo von Hoffmanstahl, librettist for Richard Strauss's *Der Rosenkavalier* and other operas, had written scenarios. But Germany, unlike England, France or America, had few great novelists at a time when the cinema was adopting the style of the narrative novel rather than the less flexible conventions of the theatre. When outstanding German films did appear after 1918 they showed many of the characteristics of stage plays, interwoven with the mystery and terror of medieval legend and the introspection of the new psychoanalytical theories of Freud and Jung.

The most notable German films of 1919–20 were historical dramas directed by Ernst Lubitsch, later to migrate to America and become a master of sophisticated Hollywood comedies and dramas. *Madame Dubarry,* starring the Polish actress Pola Negri and Emil Jannings, was an 18th-century historical drama whose unflattering portrayal of Louis XV and French society was a feeble revenge for defeat in the war. *Ann Boleyn,* in which

Jannings played Henry VIII, treated England and the Tudor monarch in a similar way. But these films were not markedly different in style and technique from those of other nations. *The Cabinet of Dr Caligari,* released in February 1920, was the first characteristically Weimar story of horror and madness. The film, still a regular feature of Film Society programmes, tells the story of a hypnotist, Dr Caligari (a name picked from the letters of Stendhal), who compels his medium to murder his enemies in authority. It begins and ends in an asylum and is photographed against studio sets which are deliberately dis-

Ernst Lubitsch, the great German director, joins the ranks of Hollywood

torted and artificial, the products of an artist's imagination, breaking completely away from any pretence at reproducing reality. *Caligari* is a filmed nightmare. Two years later Fritz Lang's *Dr Mabuse the Gambler* told a similar story of a madman's revenge on society, although the realistic backgrounds contrasted with the neuroticism of the characters. Lang, an architect and an artist by training, indulged his taste for fantasy in his recreation of the Teutonic legend of the Niebelungen Lied, an old German ballad used fifty years earlier by Richard Wagner for his Ring cycle of operas. Lang made his film in two parts, *The Death of Siegfried* and *Kriemhild's Revenge*, in 1923–4. This was followed in 1926 by *Metropolis,* a science fiction revolt of the workers against their industrial masters, reflecting the fears for the future of mankind that were disturbing the British novelists Aldous Huxley (*Brave New World*) and H. G. Wells (*The Shape of Things to Come*). Lang's catastrophe, however, ends happily with the reconciliation of capital and labour. Seven years later Hitler attempted such a reconciliation in the Nazi state but dedicated the state to a programme of Aryan supremacy and conquest.

The Aryan hero Siegfried (Paul Richter) in Fritz Lang's The Death of Siegfried, *the first part of* Die Niebelungen

These excursions into the realm of the sinister imagination were totally unlike the contemporary products of the American cinema, which concentrated mainly on realistic drama, historical adventure stories, high-speed comedy or the wholesome struggles of the Westerns. Although the themes of the German films were not imitated by Hollywood, their technical skill and imaginative direction were much admired. The Berlin studios were also producing more conventional films, most of them as trivial and meretricious as the average American product. Film historians looking back to Germany and the Soviet Union in the 1920s often recall only the culturally significant pictures and forget that these countries too produced their quota of celluloid trash. Unlike the Hollywood trash it was reserved for home consumption. Only the better German and Russian films reached foreign screens. Nearly all the American features were exported and their mediocrity was given worldwide exposure. Although not every German film was a masterpiece, the outstanding ones portrayed human tragedies with a subtlety and psychological understanding equalled by only a few American films – many of which (*Greed, The Wind, The Docks of New York*) were directed by Europeans. Both *The Last Laugh* (directed by Murnau) and *Variety* (by Dupont) starred Emil Jannings as a middle-aged man reduced to despair. *The Joyless Street,* in which G. W. Pabst directed two great Scandinavian actresses, Asta Nielsen and Greta Garbo, contrasted the flamboyant wealth of profiteers with the misery and destitution of an ordinary middle-class family during the post-war inflation. The camera moved relentlessly through scenes of jealousy, hunger and humiliation in hotels, circuses and food queues, and recorded a beautiful, disturbing picture of Germany between the Second Reich of Wilhelm II and the Third Reich of Hitler.

These silent films of the 1920s gave the German industry for a brief period a predominance which it has never regained or even attempted to regain. Their themes, however, were limited in range, concerning themselves mainly with mystery, legend and emotional dramas, and were almost entirely shot within the studio walls. Apart from the snow and mountain films of Dr Arnold Fanck (assisted by Leni Riefenstahl, who later directed such Nazi propaganda films as *Triumph of the Will*), they made few excursions into the German towns and countryside. Comedy or even the hint of laughter is rare in the films of Weimar

Leni Riefenstahl in an early German snow epic

Germany. The sardonic humour of George Grosz, the cartoonist, and Bertolt Brecht, the playwright, had few parallels in silent German films.

Denmark and Sweden had produced films before 1914 and their output expanded during the war to satisfy the markets of the Central Europe cut off from the movies produced in France, Britain and the United States. After 1918 Carl Dreyer in Denmark and Victor Sjöstrom and Mauritz Stiller in Sweden directed films of outstanding beauty and human interest. Carl Dreyer moved to France and chose a French theme – *The Passion of Joan of Arc* – for his greatest achievement in 1927. This film concentrates on the faces of the heroine, played by Maria Falconetti, and her persecutors. The tragic story of the Maid of Orleans is told as a silent conflict between Joan and her remorseless captors and contrasts vividly with the torrent of words in Bernard Shaw's play written four years earlier. The Swedish films, unlike most of those from Germany, made extensive use of outdoor shots; the sea, the woods, the hazy beauty of the Scandinavian landscape were images that were to recur in the films of Ingmar Bergman thirty years later. Sjöstrom himself reappears in Bergman's films (notably as the old doctor in *Wild Strawberries*) having given up directing after a brief and comparatively unsuccessful career in Hollywood. Stiller also went to Hollywood, with the actress Greta Garbo, whom he had discovered working as a shopgirl in Stockholm. He made only two films and died in Sweden in 1928.

But Scandinavian films were muted, in a minor key, and made only a limited impact on the development of the art of the film. Soviet films burst on the world and on the industry like a bombshell. *Battleship Potemkin* was a greater and even more startling achievement than *The Great Train Robbery* or *The Birth of a Nation*. The director, Eisenstein, showed how to use the camera to assault the audience. He combined pictorial images with a varied rhythm of cutting from one shot to another to tell a story with all the horror, beauty and dramatic power of a play by Shakespeare. Eisenstein used a hundred different shots in rapid succession to tell part of his story where an American or European director might have used ten. Edison and Lumière had made pictures move; Griffith had exploited the camera's mobility; now Eisenstein added to Griffith's technique of cutting from one episode to another by cutting the film repeatedly within one episode to concentrate attention on significant details to build up the total effect. Rachel Low has contrasted the methods of Eisenstein and the British Cecil Hepworth:

Hepworth's *Coming thro' the Rye* of 1923 makes much of the heroine's walk in the sunny fields of ripening grain, which was to be accompanied in the cinema by the music of the song. Yet despite excellent photography the few straightforward long takes of this field, seen without the music, lack anything to sustain the interest. It is interesting to imagine Eisenstein's handling of such a scene at the same date, with a multitude of shots of the rye field, the sunny sky and the birds, the grain, shadows, and all the background of changing nature which is implicit in the heroine's memory of meeting her lover, in the same field, at a different time of the year. [1]

Stalinist Russia, which later stifled its artists, writers and musicians into the unimaginative mould of socialist realism, created in its early days, seemingly by chance, a school of film-makers who could make great works of art that were also effective political propaganda. They were given financial backing and technical resources which rivalled in scale, if not in complexity and sophistication, those of Hollywood. No production costs have ever been quoted for the epics of Eisenstein and Pudovkin, but *Battleship Potemkin, The End of St Petersburg,* or *Storm over Asia,* if made in the West, would surely have cost almost as much as *Intolerance* or *Ben Hur.* Soviet films were of such high quality not only because they were made by masters of the medium but because their directors were given almost unlimited time and manpower, neither of which had to be costed by a capitalist accountant. Once made they were guaranteed distribution throughout the State-

An image of repression from Pudovkin's The End of St Petersburg

controlled cinemas. Soviet studios were still unable to produce popular mass entertainment equal to that of Hollywood, and the few American films that reached Russia in the 1920s delighted the workers in Moscow, Kiev and Odessa as much as they did those in Pittsburgh, Manchester or Milan.

Some films had been made in Russia before 1917 but the Revolution and the Civil War dispersed the film-makers. Many of these settled in France. In 1919 one company, finding it impossible to continue with its work at Yalta in the Crimea, migrated to Paris with thirty completed or half-completed films, and continued its operations as the Paris Société Ermolieff Cinéma at Montreuil. During the struggle the early studios, cameras and lights were destroyed and Russia was left in 1920 pitifully short of equipment and even of film stock. Raw film at this time was not made in Russia and could not be imported in any quantity until after the Rapallo Treaty of 1922 had re-established diplomatic and trade relations with Germany. The film industry recovered as slowly as any other Russian activity from the collapse of organized society during the up-heaval of 1917–21. Seven full-length films were made in 1921, nine in 1922, eleven in 1923, followed by a rapid rise to forty-six in 1924, sixty-eight in 1926 and 104 in 1928, a total which was not surpassed until 1958.

Sergei Eisenstein's first major film was *Strike* (1924). The technique was tentative, the film an inconclusive mixture of small-scale human narrative and a larger documentary treat-ment of industrial conflict in Tsarist society, but it was made with astonishing power and imagination and with moments of humour which become all too rare in the later classic era of Soviet cinema. Eisenstein was born in Riga on the Baltic in 1898. He grew up in a cultured middle-class family and had for many years an English nanny. Like Fritz Lang he was half-trained as an artist and architect, but the Civil War interrupted his career. He served as a soldier in the Red Army at the same time as his father was in the ranks of the counter-revolutionary White Army. After the war he entered the theatre as a designer and producer for the Central Moscow Theatre of the Proletkult. These early experiences in the world of Meyerhold and Maya-kovsky implanted in him the urge to create challenging dramatic statements and propaganda. The theatre and cinema must disturb as well as entertain. Equally important was his discovery of the picture-building structure of Oriental languages during his military service. In his films he employed separate pictures as bricks placed side by side to create an effect greater than the sum total of the individual images. Eisenstein's debt to Eastern culture increased after the visit of the Japanese Kabuki Theatre troupe of Ichikawa Sadanji to Moscow in 1928 revealed to him their rhythmic ritualistic style of acting.

Strike was followed a year later by *Battleship Potemkin,* one of the most renowned films of all time and still included in most critics' list of 'Ten Best Films'. A poll conducted among international critics in 1958 at the time of the Brussels World Exhibition put *Battleship Potemkin* clearly at the top of the list, followed by Chaplin's *Gold Rush,* with Carl Dreyer's *The Passion of Joan of Arc* fourth, Von Stroheim's *Greed* sixth, *Intolerance* seventh and Pudovkin's *Mother* eighth, five silent films in the first eight. In a similar poll organized in 1971 by *Sight and Sound,* a magazine published by the British Film Institute, *Battleship Potemkin* was third, *The Passion of Joan of Arc* seventh and Buster Keaton's *The General* eighth. *The Gold Rush* had dropped to eleventh and *Greed* and *Intolerance* were no longer listed.

Battleship Potemkin was produced as part of the Soviet celebrations for the twentieth anniversary of the 1905 Revolution in Russia, a revolution which had shaken but not dislodged the Tsarist autocracy. The film was based on an episode in that revolution. Oppressed sailors in the Tsarist Black Sea Fleet, disgusted by their poor food and the harsh discipline imposed by their officers, mutiny, take over their ship and are welcomed by the inhabitants of the Black Sea port Odessa. These episodes are told in a mixture of long and short sequences building up the tension among the ratings, exploding into revolt, and opening out into their joyful reception in port. Counter-revolution appears with the remorseless tread of Cossack troops moving down the great steps, firing volleys of shots at the civilians fleeing before them. The contrast between the disciplined descent of the soldiers and the terrified chaotic flight of their victims is portrayed by Eisenstein in a multitude of images as exciting and poignant as the music of Beethoven or Berlioz. (The special musical score composed by Edmund Meisel for Potemkin's presentation in Berlin was considered by the German authorities to be even more dangerous than the film itself.) The vivid precise impact of every shot and the alternating rhythm produced by skilful cutting represented a new use of the cinema more dramatic and urgent than anything Griffith had created. After the massacre the story moves back to the battleship awaiting attack from oncoming Tsarist ships. A mood of fear and suspense is created with longer, slower cutting from one shot to another. The scenes of gun crews waiting anxiously are replaced by shots of laughing sailors waving from the rigging as the Tsarist ships sail by and signify that they have joined the revolution.

Battleship Potemkin was great cinema and great propaganda for the Communist cause. *October,* Eisenstein's next film, this time celebrating the tenth anniversary of the successful 1917 Revolution, was almost equally impressive. Contrasting film sequences were skilfully used to create an emotional response in the viewers – sympathy for, and identification with, the revolutionaries, and contempt for their opponents. Eisenstein described this technique, called 'montage', as the cinematic equivalent of the Hegelian-Marxist dialectic, in which a thesis opposed by an antithesis merges to form a synthesis of the two ideas. In the cinema, Eisenstein wrote, 'two film pieces of any kind, placed together, inevitably combine into a new concept, a new quality, arising out of that juxtaposition'.[2] A shot of Kerensky, followed by a shot of a statue of Napoleon, implies that Kerensky himself has Napoleonic ambitions. *October* reconstructed the triumph of the Bolsheviks in Petrograd with all the excitement of an adventure story and with the moral conviction of a political pamphlet. The intensity of the images, the skill of the camera work by Edward Tisse, and the cutting by Eisenstein himself produced films as startling in their impact as the early novels of Hemingway.

Eisenstein directed only one other silent film, *The General Line,* in 1929. After this he was able to complete only two sound films, *Alexander Nevsky* (1938) and *Ivan the Terrible* (in two parts, 1944 and 1946). Seldom has such a small artistic output produced such a mighty reputation. The British novelist E. M. Forster is highly regarded on the basis of six novels but in the world of the cinema Eisenstein is a Goethe or a Shakespeare and not an E. M. Forster.

The General Line was a romantic, dramatic treatment of an unpromising theme, the formation of a collective farm and the disasters which befall its bull and its tractor. The international reputation of Eisenstein's work was strengthened by the force of his personality and the brilliance of his theoretical expositions of the art of the cinema during his visits to Britain, France and America in 1929–30. He produced almost as many books about films as films themselves. His lectures at the State Institute of Cinema in Moscow in the 1930s elaborated a philosophy of film-making more complete than that of any American director with ten times the number of films to his credit. Eisenstein was one of the first, and one of the few, great intellectuals to create great films. His films were the product of conscious thought and theoretical study, not created by dramatic instinct, as were those of Griffith, or the product of miming, stagecraft and the observation of human behaviour as were those of Chaplin. Ivor Montagu suggests that the abundance of theoretical writing about film-making produced by Eisenstein, Pudovkin and other Soviet directors and teachers is a by-product of their frustration in the early 1920s at the limitations imposed by the scarcity of film stock. They could produce only a few films and so had more time to talk about the films they hoped to create. In Hollywood commercial pressure led to films being made as rapidly as possible in order to keep the expensive studios and technicians fully employed. John Grierson, a pioneer British documentary film producer, was disappointed when he reached Hollywood in 1926, the Mecca of the film world, and found that nobody theorized about the cinema:

I had imagined that I would find there a set of adventurers, men young and eager, in a young and eager popular art, working by day and planning and plotting by night … But not on your life. The limousines flashed by on the boulevards and the sun was hot and flannels were white, and everything was for the best in the best of all bourgeois worlds … I missed something. I missed the fever that goes with creative work.[3]

Mary Pickford and Douglas Fairbanks visited Moscow in 1926, were overwhelmed by *Battleship Potemkin* and took a print back to Hollywood. Later, Ivor Montagu relates, Sam Goldwyn insisted: 'Please tell Mr Eisenstein that I have seen his film *Potemkin* and admire it very much. What we should like would be for him to do something of the same kind, but rather cheaper, for Ronald Colman.'[4] By then Eisenstein had wasted several months in America trying to get approval for the scenario of a film he was to make, and he drifted off to Mexico for further disillusion before his return to Russia and the second period of his career spent teaching and later directing the sound films of *Alexander Nevsky* and *Ivan the Terrible.* Eisenstein had begun his artistic career in the theatre and one of his last achievements was a production of Wagner's *Die Walküre* at the Bolshoi Theatre in November 1940 shortly before the German invasion. When he returned to the studio for *Ivan the Terrible* he brought with him an operatic opulence and introspection unknown in his other films. Much of *Ivan the Terrible* consists of debates within the castles or costumed processions and set pieces which could be readily transposed to the Covent Garden stage. It is impossible to imagine any American director of the 1920s as an operatic producer except perhaps Cecil B. DeMille. The Russian school brought a different type of talent into the cinema.

Vertov, Pudovkin and Dovzhenko were the greatest of a group of other Soviet directors. Their themes were similar to those of Eisenstein. Pudovkin based *Mother* on a Gorky novel about the development of a revolutionary martyr and his family; *The End of St Petersburg* was Pudovkin's version of the 1917 Revolution, while *Storm over Asia* concerned the Civil War in the Far East. Dovzhenko's *Arsenal* and *Earth* are titles evocative in themselves. These films are more concerned with individuals than the group stories of Eisenstein, but possess the same visual power and combination of moral and political messages. This was not commercial cinema, and although the films were shown to semi-literate mass audiences in Russia and could entertain as well as indoctrinate, in the West they interested only intellectual and politically sympathetic audiences. Even the less exalted Russian films were often political tracts rather than human interest stories, recalling the outburst of the heroine of

A three-screen image from Abel Gance's Napoleon, *portraying the conquest of northern Italy*

Romanov's short story *Without Cherry Blossom* – 'For us love does not exist; we have sexual relations.' It is not surprising that Russian audiences enjoyed the light relief of those American films that did reach their screens.

There was no such lack of human interest in French films. But the country that had produced some of the earliest and many of the best pre-war films failed to recover a leading position after 1918. Abel Gance made a vivid anti-war film *J'accuse* in 1919 and a powerful tragedy *La Roue* in 1923, in which trains and railway lines provided a background for human jealousies and conflict. But his most spectacular attempt to develop the art of the cinema was *Napoléon,* shown in 1927. For some sections of this film he used three screens, with at times three different film images. *Napoléon,* like *Intolerance,* is not completely convincing, but even its failure opened up new lines of investigation for the development of the cinema.

René Clair and Jacques Feyder, the latter Belgian by origin although most of his silent films were made in France, directed films which were much more successful commercially and which brought French vitality and wit to the cinema. René Clair's

A scene from René Clair's most famous comedy, An Italian Straw Hat

Italian Straw Hat was based on a famous farce by Labiche but was even faster and funnier than the stage original. As a comedy of manners it was also more formal and sophisticated than the great work of Chaplin, Buster Keaton and Harold Lloyd. Clair's style anticipated the smart Hollywood comedies of the 1930s such as *My Man Godfrey* and *Bringing up Baby*, a style which became peculiar to the cinema and had no literary or dramatic equivalent.

Although comparatively few great films emerged from France in the 1920s, Paris became the leading centre for the intellectual study of the cinema. Film reviews had appeared well before the First World War. Early in the century trade journals were published about films on offer to exhibitors, and were soon followed by film magazines satisfying the public's interest in the personal lives of the stars. In America in 1908 *The Dramatic Mirror* began to review films and in 1909 a daily newspaper, *The New York Morning Telegraph*, started a regular film column. French and English papers soon followed suit. But the early reviews consisted largely of a summary of the story and made little attempt at critical evaluation. This first appeared in France when writers such as Louis Aragon, André Breton, Ricciotto Canudo (Italian by birth but Parisian by adoption), Louis Delluc, Jean Epstein and Leon Moussinac began to discuss the nature of film art. Louis Delluc wrote the first serious film reviews in *Paris-Midi* and founded the Ciné Club in January 1920. This group wrote about films, made films and argued about films. Their admiration for the work of the Russian directors was a mixture of artistic appreciation and left-wing political sentiment. They were anxious to destroy the image of the cinema as nothing more than a glorified nickelodeon show, entertainment for the uncritical masses, and they discussed its form, artistic content and social significance. However, this hostility to the commercial attitude of the big companies and distributors was over-emphatic and lost sight of the fact that the cinema as a popular art must sell its wares to a mass market if it is to survive and fulfil its function. Such anti-commercialism has bedevilled much subsequent critical discussion of the movies. Panofsky suggests that 'while it is true that commercial art is always in danger of ending up as a prostitute, it is equally true that non-commercial art is always in danger of ending up as an old maid'.[5]

To satisfy the growing specialist market of 'cinéastes' art

cinemas were opened up such as the Théatre du Vieux Colombier, Studio 28 and Studio des Ursulines. They showed the most interesting new feature and non-commercial movies. They also revived the older films which had appeared for a few weeks or months and then vanished from the normal outlets. For the

Cover of an early film magazine

film company executives of the 1920s there was nothing so dead as last year's pictures. They were forgotten beneath the pile of new reels which issued from the studios every month. It was very difficult to be a film historian or a comparative film critic since the films themselves disappeared as quickly as stage plays do now. But stage plays can be read in book form: film scenarios were not available in the 1920s. Also, stage plays are revived in new productions using the same text and can be judged again as living drama. The remakes of old film plots which occasionally took place in the silent era were in fact totally new creations.

It is difficult for people interested in the cinema today to appreciate the extent to which films were an immediate experience fifty years ago. A feature which was missed during its normal commercial release could rarely be seen again except by travelling some distance to catch it on a more remote circuit. Its life-span would last from the time of 'first run' showing in the big city theatre on through its suburban and rural releases, but once this cycle was completed it was unlikely to reappear. We now live in an age when it is possible to enjoy the whole repertoire of film history from the early historic period through the great silent era into the complete 'talkie' output. Many films have disappeared, but a large number have been preserved for exhibition at Film Society programmes. Movies made since the 1930s are shown on television networks, and the average television viewer can gain an impression of the film achievements of the past forty years which was denied to the most ardent enthusiast in 1926 or even 1946. The surge of interest in film history within the last decade springs partly from the fact that the average man or woman can now see the material which makes, and which was made by, that history. The French art cinemas began this cult of the movie, showing Russian films together with the experimental work of writers and artists which linked the medium with the surrealist theory of the time. In 1928 Luis Bunuel made *Un Chien Andalou* with Salvador Dali. Cinema was spoken of as a new, the seventh, art, and film clubs and specialist magazines appeared. The medium used by Lumière and Edison to show trains arriving at a station and babies eating their dinner became high-brow and tackled complex, symbolic themes.

Hollywood remained unmoved by this development. Its

A severed hand in the surrealist film Un Chien Andalou *by Luis Bunuel and Salvador Dali (1928)*

directors were firmly under the control of producers, themselves under the control of financial backers, who regarded the cinema as an investment like any other. But amidst the welter of commercial trash which it produced each year were a handful of great films, some of which are discussed in Chapter 7. Even the average 'B' films from the Los Angeles studios were made to consistently high technical standards guaranteed by the professionalism of the studio teams.

English intellectuals also discovered the cinema. In 1923 the Cambridge Kinema Club was formed by Peter Le Neve Foster, and Cedric Belfrage was soon helping to run it. A few years later a report on *The Film in National Life* commented that 'A Fellow of an Oxford College no longer feels an embarrassed explanation to be necessary when he is recognized leaving a cinema'.[6] As in Paris many of these early enthusiasts supported progressive political movements as well as progressive art forms. Ivor Montagu and Hugh Miller founded the Film Society in London in 1925 with monthly shows at the New Gallery, Regent Street. They were helped by Iris Barry, one of the first regular English newspaper film critics, and the Society's sponsors

Ramsay MacDonald and Cabinet colleagues watch a film of themselves at the New Gallery Cinema in London. Next to the Labour Prime Minister is his daughter; next to Bernard Shaw (behind) is Lady Cynthia Mosley, wife of Sir Oswald Mosley

included distinguished figures from the political, artistic and cultural world, such as J. M. Keynes, Augustus John, Julian Huxley, Roger Fry, Bernard Shaw, H. G. Wells and Ellen Wilkinson, together with men who were to play an important part in British production and distribution like Anthony Asquith, Michael Balcon, Sidney Bernstein, George Pearson and, a few years later, Thorold Dickinson and John Grierson.

But the Film Society helped in England to create a climate of opinion which thought seriously about the medium and encouraged the early work of two directors of outstanding talent, Alfred Hitchcock and John Grierson. Hitchcock's first success came with *The Lodger:* an exciting film made from the most unlikely material, a novel by Mrs Belloc Lowndes with Ivor Novello as leading man. Novello appeared in several silent films including D. W. Griffith's *The White Rose,* made in Hollywood, and *Downhill,* also directed by Hitchcock. *Downhill* contained a classic sub-title redolent of the British cinema of the 1920s. Ivor, captain of a public school, and his friend have been breaking out to visit a blonde in the local village. She pretends to be pregnant and Ivor takes the blame (to protect

The film that launched the movie career of Ivor Novello, one of Britain's few international stars of the silent era

Novello pluckily takes the rap, in Downhill, *for besmirching local honour*

his friend of course) and is expelled. As he hears the sentence in the headmaster's study the sub-title gives his anguished response: 'Does this mean, Sir, that I won't be able to play cricket for the Old Boys?'[7]

John Grierson took his camera out of the studios to photograph men at work, and his *Drifters* (1929) presaged the British documentary films of the 1930s, sometimes overrated like a good deed in the naughty, or almost non-existent, world of native British cinema but welcome both as worthy British productions and as films of real people in real situations. They are of considerable value to the social historian of the period and will be even more valuable to future generations, who will treasure them as we would treasure film records of the early textile factories or the building of the British canals and railroads. Robert Flaherty in America with *Nanook of the North* (1922), about Eskimos, and *Moana* (1926), about South Sea islanders, had created great films drawn from factual material illustrating the lives of primitive peoples.

By the time that sound invaded the cinema in 1927–8 a new art form had thus been created in which directors used the camera to tell stories economically and effectively with pictures and only a minimum of sub-titles. Actors understood how to convey emotion without words and without exaggerated grimaces and gestures. The silent cinema, by drawing on the skills of miming, photography and brilliant set designers, by using scripts created especially for the medium, by rejoicing in the use of a mobility denied to the theatre and of pictures denied to the novelist, and by creating a visual rhythm comparable to the beat and sweep of great music, was justifying the claim that it had indeed become 'the seventh art'.

| CHAPTER FOUR | Movies become big business |

Films were not primarily or even predominantly an art form. They were a business producing mass entertainment. Most of the men and women who worked in the business were out to make money, not works of art. Even the directors, writers and actors who were concerned about aesthetic standards were dependent on an army of technicians and supporting staff for whom the wage packet was all-important. Film-making is a group activity, and an expensive one. Money must be found before the first scene can be shot. An artist, a composer or a poet can live and work in a garret, using comparatively cheap materials, and still produce a masterpiece. Even if the public never sees, hears or reads their work, it still exists and may one day receive the recognition that most artists seek. But films must be seen quickly if they are to recover their costs of production and produce the profit expected by the men or institutions who have invested in them. The profits were often large and their expectation attracted capital into the business to finance studios, distributing agencies, picture palaces. The story of the birth of the movies is the story of the birth of an industry, a chapter of economic as well as cultural history.

'Just as McCormick solved the problem of wholesale farming by the invention of the harvester machine, so Edison and Eastman solved the problem of the wholesale manufacture of amusement by the motion picture and its retailing at prices within the reach of all,' Morton Sills, a film actor, told students at the Harvard Business School in one of a series of lectures organized in 1927 by film financier Joseph Kennedy (father of President J. F. Kennedy).[1] The lecture series brought academic recognition to Joe Kennedy, whose grandfather had fled penniless from Ireland in the 'hungry forties'. It also brought recognition of the economic importance and job opportunities of the film industry from the leading American university business school, a training ground for the aristocracy of Wall Street.

From their earliest days films were potentially big money-makers. With primitive equipment, outdoor locations and unpaid workers and bystanders who appeared rather than acted before the cameras, a film could be produced cheaply; dozens of copies could be made and sold for twenty times the cost of production, initially to music halls or travelling showmen who needed only a projector, screen and a few chairs. In the theatre or music hall performers had to be paid for each performance. Films could be shown over and over again to paying audiences for the mere cost of projection. But the big profits, even in the early days of the cinema, accrued to the exhibitors rather than to the makers of films. The latter sold their prints at low prices to showmen, who reaped the benefits of multiple exhibition and sometimes earned a bonus by making their own copies of the film and selling them with no return to the original makers.

Hollywood comes to Batavia (modern Jakarta) in the Dutch East Indies

The nickelodeons, opened in 1905, were the first attempts to capitalize on a mass market by giving twenty or thirty shows a day at five cents a seat to large audiences. With the nickelodeons specialization entered the industry and the middle man, the distributor, appeared. Distributors bought the films from the makers and, instead of selling them outright to exhibitors, rented them out for a day or a week to showmen and then passed them on around the country collecting their percentage on every transaction. The distributors were backed by capital resources larger than those of the small-scale nickelodeon proprietors or even of most early film-makers. It is true that Edison's operations were supported by the General Electric Company and the Pierrepont Morgan banking house. Harriman and Empire Trust (Rockefeller) money was invested in the rival Biograph Company. But these were the exceptions. Most early film-makers had little capital other than that invested in their cameras and equipment. They were at the mercy of the distributors who bought up the films and sometimes advanced money for future productions. These distributors began to control the industry. They eventually expanded back into production and forward into exhibition, creating the great companies of the industry, Paramount, Metro-Goldwyn-Mayer, Fox and Universal, who owned film stars, writers, studios, distribution agencies and picture palaces. Fifty years later most of these great companies have been swallowed up by the giant financial 'conglomerates' of the 1960s, for whom movie-making is only one activity in a whole range of money-making concerns. The 'moguls' of the 1920s, Zanuck, Mayer, Laemmle, Fox, were anxious to make money but they were also anxious to make films and were personally involved in studio production. For them movies were big business, but it was their only major business. Now the companies are run by executives and analysts who may never have heard the crack of a clap board. Today Paramount in a good year produces only 16% of the earnings of its parent company Gulf and Western. Universal is controlled by the Music Corporation of America, and Twentieth-Century Fox by the Trans-America Corporation. Metro-Goldwyn-Mayer remains independent, but is becoming increasingly interested in hotel and property operations. Warner Brothers has grown into Warner Communications, selling sheet music and gramophone records as well as pictures.

All the companies have drastically curtailed their studio operations and are selling off the vast estates they bought for location work.

In 1910, however, the great American film corporations had yet to be built. The growing point was still distribution; the middle-men, the wholesalers of films, came out on top. In France, however, the first leaders in the industry, Lumière and Pathé, were production companies and also substantial manufacturers of photographic equipment for both movie and 'still' cameras. This provided a broader base for their studio operations. Star Film of Méliès was the first major company to concentrate on production. Pathé later expanded from equipment into the manufacture of raw film stock. By 1914 Pathé were selling 80 per cent of all the projectors in the world and were challenging Eastman-Kodak's position as the major manufacturer of photographic stock. They had opened branches in New York, Berlin, Moscow, London and Singapore.

Léon Gaumont, another manufacturer of equipment, built up a major production company in France by dint of his tough personal supervision. Like earlier giants of the industrial revolution he waited at the factory door each morning to check in his staff, including directors and actors. His attitude to the film-making business anticipated the production schedules of the Hollywood studios of the 1920s.

Both Pathé and Gaumont made substantial profits. In 1901 only fifteen copies of a five-minute film needed to be sold to recover the costs of production, and frequently over 300 were marketed. Pathé's profits of 421,000 francs in 1901–2 rose to over two and a half million in 1905–6 and to eight million in 1912–13. In ten years the value of the original shares worth 100 francs had increased to 1200 francs. Some of this capital had been provided by outside backers including Jean Neyret, president of mining and steel companies and a director of the Crédit Lyonnais Bank. Gaumont became a public company in 1906, supported by a Franco-Swiss Bank. Lumière and Méliès lacked the financial skill to develop their companies in this way and were soon left far behind. French studios in 1914 provided nearly three-quarters of all the film exports in the world, but France's predominantly pre-industrial peasant economy was an inadequate base from which to maintain this supremacy. The home market was limited, with only 1200 cinemas compared to

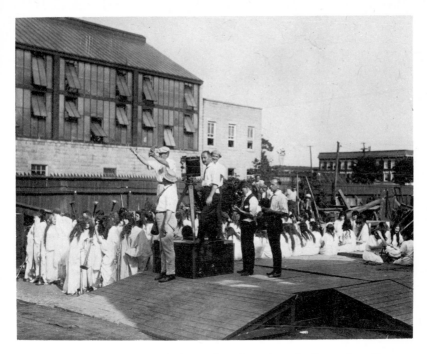

Assembling an outdoor scene, with chorus of angels, at the early Vitagraph studio

2500 in Germany, 4500 in Britain, and over four times that number in America.

Production was severely restricted after August 1914, dropping from 9000 metres to 4075 metres a week by 1916, and the French lead disappeared. Pathé were forced to sell their US business to Merrill Lynch and the French and American Pathé companies combined with Dupont to manufacture raw film in competition with Eastman-Kodak. But by the following year Charles Pathé made a deal with Eastman to avoid bankruptcy, accepted a 50 per cent American participation in his firm, and became one of the early victims of the Wall Street domination of the industry. A year later America supplied 98 per cent of the world's film exports and built up a commanding position which was never subsequently challenged. By 1923 France was only the fifth largest producer in the world, outranked by the United States, Germany, Japan and Russia, and only 10 per cent of the films shown on French screens were home products compared with 85 per cent from Hollywood. In 1913 America exported 32 million feet of film and imported 16 million feet. Ten years later the figures were 146 and 9 million feet respectively. In the following two years imports dropped to a little over 7 million while exports climbed to 178 and eventually in 1929 to 282 million feet. Thirty-five per cent of these features went to Britain, the rest to all the continents of the world.

No other challenge was offered to the rise of the American cinema industry. Italy had established a market for its epic films of the 1911–15 era, but its output was much smaller than that of France and was drastically curtailed when Italy declared war in April 1915. Italian cinema went into a cultural and economic decline from which it did not emerge until the end of the Second World War thirty years later. Great Britain had more cinemas but produced fewer films than France and Italy, and depended on imports for a major part of its screen programmes even before 1914. Denmark, Sweden, Germany and Russia produced films but on a limited scale. 450 of the 500 feature films screened in Denmark in 1925 were American. Japanese studios were opening up and in the 1920s were producing some five hundred films a year. However their tales of medieval Japan, employing the ritual and techniques of the Japanese theatre, were of little interest abroad, except in China. Even in 1929 at the end of the silent era only one Japanese film was exported to France and the United States, and Japanese cinema remained virtually unknown in the West until the 1950s.

From its earliest days the American industry expanded rapidly. By 1908 nearly 10,000 nickelodeons were creating an insatiable demand for films. In 1907 the Kalem Company was formed with a capital of 600 dollars; a few years later it was producing three films a week and an annual profit of over 250,000 dollars. Belatedly Edison and his early associates realized they were sitting on top of a gold mine. They now fought to bring it under their exclusive control.

Under Edison's leadership nine leading manufacturers and distributors with a miscellaneous collection of patents for camera and projection equipment banded together to form a monopoly trust to shut out all their competitors. They established the Motion Picture Patents Company (MPPC) on 1 January 1909. At this period cartels or trusts were being formed in many sectors of American industry. Eastman-Kodak co-operated with the MPPC and agreed to sell raw film stock to trust members only. The company planned to force exhibitors

In 1909 an International Film Congress met in Paris to attempt to establish a patent control similar to that of the MPPC in the USA. Circled (left to right) are Charles Pathé, George Eastman, Georges Méliès and Léon Gaumont

to obtain a licence at two dollars a week. The licence would give them the right to show the films produced by the MPPC companies. They alleged that their control over the patent rights for cameras and projectors would prevent any other groups from making films legitimately. Once the monopoly was established rental charges could be raised and the gold mine could be exploited.

But American capitalism spawned enterprising trust breakers as well as trust makers. Producers and distributors outside the ring were not overawed by the flimsy legal rights of the MPPC and were determined to make and distribute their own films. Small companies, using unlicensed equipment, flitted from one location to another, pursued by the MPPC's private detectives. Despite this harassment the independent companies prospered, and two of them, Fox and Universal, became leading motion picture companies of the twenties and thirties. Both William Fox and Carl Laemmle (the founder of Universal Pictures) saw the advantages of combining in one company the three major aspects of the movie business – making films in their own studios, distributing them through their own renting companies, and exhibiting them in their own cinemas. Small-scale specialized activities were being absorbed into vertically integrated companies similar to the developments in big industries such as iron and steel, where great firms like Krupps or Bethlehem Steel owned iron and coal mines, iron foundries, steel works, manufacturing plants and shipyards.

The election of Woodrow Wilson as President of the United States in 1912 brought to the White House an administration eager to challenge monopoly positions in American business. The legality of the MPPC's position was taken to the Law Courts in 1912 and the Company was destroyed by 1917. The battle was not entirely one of Fox as David challenging Edison as Goliath, since Fox himself was backed by a group of New Jersey financiers headed by John F. Dryden, President of the mighty Prudential Insurance Company. William Randolph Hearst, a dominant figure in the American newspaper industry, had invested in the International Film Company and later the Universal Company. Hearst continued his association with the movies into the 1920s, financing the production of films

Marion Davies as a young girl, in her early film days, and later as a star with Louis B. Mayer and Mr and Mrs Will Hays (opposite)

starring his protegée Marion Davies and squandering on them almost as much money as he poured into his other megalomaniac extravagances such as San Simeon, the vast palace and estate he created on the Pacific Coast north of Los Angeles. The movies took their revenge in 1940 when Orson Welles created *Citizen Kane*, a fictional film based on Hearst's life story and with a central character, a newspaper proprietor played by Orson Welles, as arrogant and opinionated as Hearst himself. In the film, regarded by most critics today as certainly one of the ten best movies of all time, the fictional hero lavishes money trying to promote a career for his mistress as an opera singer,

not a movie star, but the parallel with Hearst's underwriting of Marion Davies's appearances is very marked. Marion Davies undoubtedly performed much more competently before the camera than Kane's mistress did on the operatic stage, and eventually her films were less disastrous than many of the other business activities of Randolph Hearst. His chain of newspapers across the United States constantly praised her films, but almost immediately after his death in 1951 the instructions to his editors to mention Miss Davies at least once each day were dropped as soon as his wife and family took control of the company.

William Fox, a leading protagonist in the fight of the 'independents' against the MPPC, prospered in the 1920s and for a brief period promised to become the greatest individual in the business. But he was forced into liquidation in 1931 when he had over-extended himself in the early days of the talkies and become caught in the backwash of the 1929 Depression.

Universal and Fox, the biggest independent companies challenging the MPPC, were joined by Famous Players–Lasky,

William Fox first challenged the MPPC as a cinema owner and distributor, but as he gained confidence he established his own studio, shown here at Fort Lee, New Jersey, the typical confused mixture of glasshouse indoor stages and outdoor lots

a group formed in 1916 by Adolph Zukor, Jesse Lasky, Samuel Goldwyn and Cecil B. DeMille, whose work was distributed by the Paramount Picture Company. In 1917 the production and distributing units were all linked in one company and Paramount became the greatest force in Hollywood in the 1920s. As the old group of MPPC companies declined, Wall Street banking firms rushed to invest money in this new industry, despite the failure of the two early stock issues of Triangle and World Film Companies. The home market was doubling every five years and the cinemas of the world welcomed American films to fill the gaps left by the decline in French and Italian production.

The film stars too began to realize that they were now operating in a big business and demanded their share of the profits. Since the difference between a successful and an unsuccessful film was several hundreds of thousands of dollars, and since success depended increasingly on the skill and personality of the leading players, these players began to force companies to bid for their services. The competition to sign up the leading stars was rather like the competition in England in the 1960s to capture the outstanding football players once the maximum wage in the professional game was abolished and clubs could bargain for the services of individual footballers. Charles Chaplin and Mary Pickford were the pace-setters and forced up their demands as much for the prestige of being the most highly paid performers as for the intrinsic value of the money itself. Mary Pickford may have been 'America's Sweetheart' but she was also the scourge of the company treasurers. In 1911 she was being paid only 175 dollars a week. In 1918 she exchanged a contract with Artcraft, which guaranteed her 500,000 dollars a year and 50 per cent of the profits, for a new one with First National offering 675,000 dollars for three pictures plus 250,000 dollars bonus, 50 per cent of the profits, and 50,000 dollars for her mother. Adolph Zukor, owner of Artcraft (a Paramount subsidiary), could not match this but offered her 250,000 dollars a year if only she would make no pictures at all. Zukor was attempting to build up a monopoly of stars. For a brief period in 1917 he seemed on the verge of success. Paramount had under contract Mary Pickford, Douglas Fairbanks, William S. Hart (the cowboy hero), Wallace Reid, John Barrymore, Billie Burke, Mae Murray,

(Left to right) Morris Geste, Adolph Zukor, Cecil B. DeMille, Jesse Lasky and Samuel Goldwyn in 1915 on the set of Temptation, *a Famous Players-Paramount production*

Adolph Zukor the young Hungarian immigrant aged eighteen and the elder statesman aged eighty, receiving a tribute from Hollywood's moral guardian, Will Hays

Sessue Hayakawa and many of the other best known performers. Zukor sought also to dominate the industry by creating a major chain of prestigious 'first run' cinemas. These were the big luxury cinemas in major cities where new films were given their first showing. Only when they had finished their run in these first-class houses were they passed on down the line to smaller and smaller cinemas in more and more remote areas. The publicity and glamour surrounding the performances at a 'first run' cinema were calculated to make audiences and owners of smaller theatres believe that if a film was shown in such a house then it must be good, or conversely if it did not open in a major 'first run' hall then it could not be worth seeing or showing.

In 1919 Paramount set out to capture the outlets, buying a major interest in Southern Enterprises Inc. with 135 theatres in southern States. A year later the New England Theatres Inc. with houses in the north-east were snapped up, and for the first time a producing and distributing company reached out directly to the box office and the theatre patrons.

Adolph Zukor began also to force exhibitors to show films for three or six days and not to change their programmes daily.

London publicity for a Chaplin film, 1918

He insisted that if they wanted the main Paramount films they must agree to show only the products of his company. He offered a package of 104 films for a year's programmes to be taken en bloc. If managers wanted to pick and choose from this range they had to pay very high prices for individual items. The policy, known as 'block booking', guaranteed showing for all Paramount films but was bitterly resented by cinema proprietors. It was also 'blind booking' since they had no chance of seeing any of the items before they arrived in the cans for showing. Jesse Lasky, as a producer, complains of the interruption caused by the need to attend sales conventions:

These annual pep rallies unquestionably proved their worth and the custom was quickly adopted by all companies in the field. However, it was a vast annoyance for us in the production department to have to take time off from the actual making of pictures to exhort the sales force to fever pitch with grandiloquent promises and incendiary teasers about the product they could expect in the twelve months' season starting in September.

We were confident that the mill would keep grinding and that the salesmen would have the required number of celluloid reels to deliver to their customers in a year or two hence, but we were often pretty fuzzy in our own minds about what would be in those reels. [2]

The new monopoly attacked the independence of the small man. The MPPC had been broken, but Paramount's bid to capture the stars and the big cinemas threatened to be equally dangerous. The Federal Trade Commission noted that 'in one week of 1920 more than 6000 American theatres, or approximately one third of all the motion pictures in the United States, showed nothing but Paramount pictures'. Moreover, they included many of the bigger, better halls, since exhibition in those 6000 meant that 'about sixty-seven cents of every dollar that was paid to enter motion picture theatres was paid to enter those theatres which displayed Paramount Pictures'. [3]

Once again a resistance group was formed, this time of exhibitors who refused to be crushed by the big companies. Thomas Tally, the pioneer cinema owner of Los Angeles, and John D. Williams of West Virginia established the First National Exhibitors' Circuit in April 1917. Soon the proprietors of over 5000 cinemas had joined in this organization to offer a defence against the power of the producers and distributors. Just as distributors had expanded into production and exhibition, so the First National Circuit moved back into production in order to break its dependence on the major film-making companies. This Exhibitors' organization would make its own films to show in its own cinemas. First National signed up Chaplin, paying him over one million dollars to make eight short comedies a year, and followed this by engaging Mary Pickford herself and director D. W. Griffith. The mad chase by the companies for talent and by the stars for money was on. The audience paid the price; seats which had cost five cents in the nickelodeon were now fifteen to thirty-five cents, and for special shows were pushed up to a dollar or two dollars. The American government took its share by imposing a 10 per cent tax on all cinema seats costing over ten cents in 1918, and the first systematic records of attendances were begun.

The end of the war, coinciding with an influenza epidemic, brought a halt to the boom. Some weaker companies went out of business. But soon the post-war expansion began and world markets were opened up to the movies from Hollywood, with their vast financial and technical resources. American companies, able to recover all the costs of their production from cinemas in their own country, could now swamp the screens of the world with their output. European producers with a far smaller domestic market could not compete at home with the scale and efficiency of Hollywood and were even less capable of persuading America to import large numbers of European films in exchange. *Choosing a Wife* with Owen Nares and Isabel Elsom was the first important full-length English film to be shown in New York. *The Times* of 13 August 1919 comments that 'managers and the public were keenly interested in seeing what British companies who complain of the flooding of the British market by American productions could do'. They were unimpressed. *The Times* reporter confessed that 'the action from the American point of view drags'. The New World took the best European stars and directors to work in California and made it even more difficult to produce European films which might secure a wide distribution in the United States.

American directors, stars, distributors and exhibitors fought to increase their share of the proceeds. Authors were hired at extravagant salaries to write scripts that were often re-written two or three times before they reached the studio floor. The crazy spendthrift era of Hollywood had begun. In an attempt to control expenditure the financiers appointed studio executive directors to supervise the film-makers and to organize the studios on the systematic mass production lines of the motor car industry. Shooting schedules were devised, budgets were tightly enforced, directors and stars were fitted into a conveyor belt system. Old campaigners resented the change. Cecil B. DeMille lamented: 'When banks came into pictures, trouble came in with them. When we operated on Wall Street money there was grief in the industry.'[4]

The three greatest stars, Mary Pickford, Charlie Chaplin and Douglas Fairbanks, the athletic lover of the screen, decided to break away from this control to make their own films. Together with D. W. Griffith they formed the United Artists Company as a distributing agency for their own producing companies. 'The lunatics have taken over the asylum,' was one Hollywood comment.

The commercial struggle continued. As the First National Company consolidated itself into a major unit, a fresh group emerged to protect the interests of the small man. In 1920 'The Motion Picture Theatre Owners' of America was formed with a

Founder members of United Artists – Fairbanks, Griffith, Pickford and Chaplin, 1919

membership of over 10,000 employing James J. Walker, a New York Senator (later to become a notorious Mayor of New York), as their spokesman and political agent. They fought to preserve the independence of the small cinema owners against the big companies and to fight the practice of 'block booking' which had now grown to such an extent that small cinemas were being forced to become 'tied houses' taking only the movies of one company.

First National and Paramount were locked in conflict. Adolph Zukor of Paramount raised ten million dollars through Kuhn Loeb and Company on Wall Street with the aid of a prospectus which showed that in 1919 the 18,000 US cinemas would receive gross receipts of 800 million dollars. This new capital was used to buy up prestige cinemas – the Rialto and Rivoli in New York, the Grauman and Rialto in Los Angeles – to break the First National's dominant position. Zukor threatened to build Paramount cinemas in every major city in direct competition with those owned by their rival company. The Federal Trade Commission investigated complaints against these practices alleging that the company had intimidated motion picture theatre owners by 'threatening to build and/or operate theatres in competition with exhibitors who refused to sell or lease their houses, and to cut off or interfere with the film service of such exhibitors'.[5] Other practices included offering higher rentals for the tenancy of cinemas or reducing the prices of admission to cinemas showing their films until any other houses in the area were forced to agree to take Paramount Films or be driven out of business.

Other powerful men appeared on the scene. Joseph Kennedy, who later served as Franklin D. Roosevelt's ambassador in London in the late 1930s, built up part of his fortune by running a group of New England cinemas he bought in 1919. A few years later he was in charge of FBO (Film Booking Office), a small producing company. FBO's main assets were the cowboy stars Tom Mix and Fred Thomson, whose horse 'Silver King' had a 25,000-dollar stable with mahogany floors and travelled in a custom-built Packard van. Kennedy's big film profits were made during the change-over to sound when he organized the raising of capital for new equipment in the studios and cinemas. He financed Gloria Swanson's ill-fated *Queen Kelly*, directed by the extravagant genius Erich von Stroheim, but eventually moved out of the film world. Gloria Swanson recalled later: 'I questioned his judgement. He did not like to be questioned.'[6]

By the mid-twenties Hollywood was controlled by eight major companies – Paramount, Universal, Fox, Loew's Inc. or Metro-Goldwyn-Mayer, Warner Brothers, First National, United Artists, and Columbia (newly created by Harry Cohn). Pathé was by now a declining force. They each produced a full-length film every week or fortnight, rolling out of the studios like products from an assembly line. Few films cost more than half a million dollars to make and most needed around two hundred thousand, despite the inflated salaries of producers and stars. This sustained, regular operation of the industry was very different from the spasmodic high cost rhythm of the American movie companies of the late sixties and early seventies. Even though 'faster' film – able to absorb more light – has sent directors out of expensive studios on to location for much of their work, films still cost millions to create and promote, tying up large amounts of capital, and can be financially disastrous if they do not capture public interest. Advertising and launching expenditure is so high that it is now frequently better business to cut the losses on an unpromising venture and leave it on the shelf. 'Taken film by film, this industry is just a dice game. Average it out, then it becomes a business', commented Douglas Netter, a Metro-Goldwyn-Mayer executive, in 1972. Fifty years earlier, apart from a few super-productions, the risks were much lower since the average costs were smaller and the major companies' control of cinemas guaranteed an outlet for most of their output.

Trouble came, however, from the Paramount attempt to gain complete supremacy. In the struggle they, and some other companies, over-extended themselves in lavish expenditure on cinemas and studios. By 1926 radio was a serious rival entertainment, keeping customers at home, and film profits slumped dramatically. Only the arrival of talking pictures saved the industry from collapse. Although sound equipment involved heavy new capital investment, the audiences flocked back into the cinemas, producing record profits in 1929 which were not exceeded again until the wartime boom years of the 1940s.

CHAPTER FIVE

Movies and society

For those whom life has cheated
Open the electric paradise

wrote the Russian poet Moravskaya.[1] This sentiment was echoed by Hugo von Hoffmanstahl, Austrian playwright and librettist: 'What people seek in the motion pictures ... what the masses of working people demand of them is a substitute for dreams. They would fill their imagination with pictures, powerful presentiments charged with the very essence of life itself.'[2] The creation of illusions to compensate their devotees for the drabness of their normal routine was one of the main social functions of the cinema, and these illusions were distributed to the largest audiences the world had ever known. The social and cultural impact of the cinema was far more widespread than that of any previous form of entertainment. It was the second of the great 20th-century mass media, preceded by popular journalism and followed by radio and television. Earlier diversions – the theatre, opera, literature – had been limited in their appeal. Even the popular entertainments of the 19th century, the music halls and burlesque theatres, could reach only a small proportion of the urban populations. As more people learnt to read at the end of the century, cheap newspapers and mass circulation magazines shaped the minds and opinions of their readers, but the cinema had an even greater and more immediate impact, especially upon the illiterate immigrant peoples of the United States. Films were cheap and easily transported, could be shown in any darkened hall or converted shop with electric power, a projector and a screen, and were readily understood and appreciated. Twenty years after the first public showings in 1895–6 the cinematograph was influencing the ideas and ambitions of a quarter of the world's population.

It is surprising that this power of the silent cinema was comparatively little used, at least overtly. The Russian Communist leaders appreciated the significance of the cinema and exploited it to convince their illiterate peasant masses of the benefits of their new system. Lenin emphasized that 'for us the cinema is the most important of all the arts'.[3] But in the capitalist world comparatively little use was made of it for political or even commercial advertisement until after 1945, when the radio and television networks were already exploiting their inroads into the minds of audiences, who could be conditioned as well as entertained. Marxists, however, would claim that the control of the cinema by private business interests, and from a very early stage predominantly by American banking houses, meant that it was used to project capitalist values to predominantly working-class audiences. The French Socialist leader Jean Jaurès predicted that the cinema would be 'the theatre of the proletariat'.[4] It did become a theatre of the proletariat but one that inculcated into them the standards of bourgeois, not Marxist, morality, despite the social criticism implicit in some early Griffith films and in the idealization of Chaplin's tramp struggling against the established order. The films of the 1920s and 1930s were made by producers and directors whose political and social views were normally well to the right of their audiences. In contrast the producers and directors of the 1960s and 1970s are often more socially critical than their customers, and their products tend to challenge rather than support contemporary society.

The content of the earliest films of the first decade had little social significance. Short descriptive, trick or humorous films could develop no substantial themes. The first impact of the medium was to provide a popular diversion devoid of any message. But the entertainment itself was socially important for the predominantly working-class audiences, especially those of the crowded American cities of New York, Pittsburgh, Chicago, Boston or Philadelphia. At a dinner given for President Woodrow Wilson by the Motion Picture Board of Trade in January 1916, J. Stuart Blackton, an early producer and director, said that the number of cheap drinking saloons in the Wilkes-Barre district of Pennsylvania had declined from over 10,000 in 1906 to 1400 in 1916. Their place, he claimed, had been taken by nickelodeons and cinemas. In 1917 a British report on *The Cinema: Its Present Position and Future Possibilities* concluded that 'we have been convinced by the amount of testimony offered in favour of its value as a cheap amusement for the masses, for the parents as well as children, especially as regards its influence in decreasing hooliganism and as a counter attraction to the public house'.[5]

This report was commissioned by the National Council for Public Morals for Great and Greater Britain, an independent organization under the Presidency of the Bishop of Birmingham and with many other churchmen and MP's from all parties among its Vice-Presidents. The Council's object was 'The Regeneration of the Race – Spiritual, Moral, Physical'. Concerned that the cinematograph might be delaying this regeneration, it established a Commission to enquire into the influences of the cinema upon society, especially upon young people. The Commission was welcomed by the Associations of Film Exhibitors and Distributors. Its members included leaders of all the main religious groups, the Chief Film Censor, Sir Robert Baden-Powell (the founder of the Boy Scouts Movement) and Dr Marie Stopes, a pioneer advocate of birth control and greater sexual freedom. Evidence was taken from forty-two witnesses varying from the Chief Constable of Edinburgh and the Head Master of Eton College to schoolchildren from Brixton and Bethnal Green. The report substantiated none of the alarming allegations that were being made about the harmful effect of the cinema on the British people, although it regretted the failure to make full use of the film's capacity to educate as well as entertain. 'The witnesses interviewed were almost unanimously of the opinion that the cinema as at present conducted is better for the child than the street' and 'better for the child than the music hall'.[6] It seemed to be regarded as better than the public house for all ages. The Chief Constable of Edinburgh was certain that 'the gradual decrease in drunkenness has been brought about by opening up to the people of more means of rational amusement such as the picture house. These places of amusement, which always seem to be well patronized by the public, have without doubt brought about a wonderful improvement in the sobriety of the city.' Unlike the theatres and music halls very few cinemas (in Anglo-Saxon countries at least) were licensed for the sale of alcohol, and their prosperity depended upon their reputation as a cheap entertainment for the whole family and especially for mothers and children.

As programmes lengthened, film stories became more important and began to reflect an attitude to the society around them. From the beginning Westerns were based on the simple themes that remained dominant for fifty years: crime does not pay and the 'good guy' always defeats the 'bad guy' in the end. Not until the 1950s did many Westerns confuse this basic message with doubts about morality, the Indian and even the sheriff. Occasionally other feature films about working-class life, common in the period 1905–15 but less frequent in 1915–55, hey-day of the bourgeois and exotic cinema in America and England, were sometimes critical of the justice and morality of the established order. Lewis Jacobs in *The Rise of the American Film* describes a number of films with titles such as *The Need of Gold, Nobody Works Like Father, The Ex-Convict,* in which the poor struggle against the temptation of poverty and are frequently victimized by the rich and established, who are themselves denounced in other films – *Crooked Banker* or *The Grafters.* But even in these socially critical films, like the Victorian melodramas which they closely resembled, honesty usually triumphed in the closing frames, or else honesty was assumed to be its own reward. The system itself was accepted as just and reasonable; doubts were cast only on the black sheep abusing the rest of the flock.

By 1915 the movies had travelled a long way from their early role as a music-hall novelty or as a diversion for predominantly working-class audiences in travelling fairs or cheap nickelodeons. They were becoming a more respectable entertainment in more luxurious cinemas whose customers were called patrons. This itself denotes a change of style, just as the current use of the term 'studio' for cinema indicates a new change of emphasis. These patrons were drawn from all classes and went to see films with themes and characters corresponding to those of the theatre of Ibsen, Pinero or Somerset Maugham, in addition to those of Victorian melodramas or music halls. Professor Marwick has pointed out that the cinema was 'exceptional among all the products of twentieth-century technology in that it reached the poorer elements of the community first before spreading upwards to those who at first affected contempt for it'.[7] But although middle-class families began to frequent picture

Fairground film shows in the first years of the century. The bottom photograph was taken at St Giles Fair, Oxford

palaces, they were still regarded mostly, in Britain at least, as peoples' palaces, just as the theatre has remained mainly a bourgeois entertainment. A statistical survey of the cinema industry in 1934 revealed that nearly half of the seats cost sixpence or less and nearly eighty per cent not more than a shilling. Over the whole of Britain there was one cinema seat for every twelve inhabitants, but this figure ranged from one for every fourteen in London and the Home Counties to one for every nine in industrial Lancashire and Scotland and for every ten in South Wales and the North of England. The cinema seats were thickest where the working-class populations were most heavily concentrated. In 1934 these seats may not have been so fully occupied but it is indicative of some pressure of working-class demand that they had been installed during the previous twenty years.[8]

Despite, perhaps because of, this factor, which was paralleled in America and Western Europe, many of the films of the 1920s featured smart middle-class heroes and heroines moving in a world of motor-cars, steamships and elegant homes, as portrayed by Ernst Lubitsch and Cecil B. DeMille. The backgrounds had to conform to a popular, Hollywood-inspired concept of affluence. D. W. Griffith, writing *Are Moving Pictures Destructive of Good Taste?* in the magazine *Arts and Decorations* in September 1923, complained that 'if a producer had the courage to show a room in a home of wealth that was not crowded with masses of misplaced magnificence he would disappoint his audiences. The producer offers such drawing rooms and interiors as the "poorer classes" like to think are the possessions of the rich.'

The stars themselves were as nouveau riche as their studio backgrounds. Most of the great Hollywood personalities who commanded six-figure salaries and lived in Beverly Hills mansions as opulent and often as artificial as their film sets – this style of domestic architecture has been called 'early marzipan' – came from homes as poor as those of the movie moguls and those of most of their fans. Douglas Fairbanks, Richard Barthelmess, William Powell were some of the few middle-class, college-educated stars in California. The rest were manufactured gems in manufactured settings, acting out dream lives for their followers both on and off the studio floor.

Compton Mackenzie encountered an even more outlandish

example of the cinema's need to gild the lily. While his novel *Sinister Street* was being filmed he went to see some of the 'rushes'.

To my consternation I was shown Lord Saxby in full regimentals of the Welsh Guards, bearskin and all, riding along a country lane to have tea with Mrs Fane.

'But look,' I protested to the two little Jewish brothers who were managing Ideal Films, 'A Colonel in the Guards would not go to tea in the country dressed up like that. He must be in mufti.'

The two Rowsons smiled.

'What you must try and understand, Mr Mackenzie, is that the cinema audience wants romance. We must give them romance. There's no romance in a suit of dittoes.'[9]

Most of the films of the 1920s delivered this romance. Their standards of behaviour and dress were the standards to which their mass audiences aspired. A post-First World War generation grew up for whom the cinema was the greatest single educational and social influence, just as the values of the post-1950 generation have been largely determined by television programmes. There is, however, one essential difference. Television programmes present a much wider range of themes, whereas the cinema of the 1920s provided a diet consisting largely of fictional fantasy, comedy or adventure. J. P. Mayer's study of *British Cinemas and their Audiences* records the confessions of this generation and the central role of the cinema in its life: 'At the age of 25 I have literally gone to the cinema all my life. I first entered the cinema (in my mother's arms) at the age of one month. I have therefore been going to the cinema for exactly a quarter of a century.'[10] And for many of this group, going to the cinema meant going regularly once or twice every week regardless of the programme. They went to be entertained and were unconsciously conditioned. By 1920 the films that conditioned them were predominantly American, since Hollywood was supreme and eighty per cent of the movies that were shown emanated from California. This influence began the standardization of life, of city life at least, which has been a significant feature of 20th-century society. The standards which have been adopted are those of the United States.

These influences have been for good and for evil. One schoolboy wrote for J. P. Mayer that since I have been going to the pictures I always touch my hat when I meet anybody. I always greet everybody with a smile. When I bump into anybody I always say I am sorry ... I have also learned to become better-mannered at the dinner table. In dress I always have a crease in my trousers. I always put grease on my hair and have a parting in it ... I always strip to the waist when I wash. I clean my teeth every morning. All these things I have imitated from the films.[11]

Sometimes the ideals proved not so easily attainable. A married woman of twenty-six grumbled: 'Do films make me dissatisfied? Definitely they do! I find myself comparing my home, my clothes, even my husband. I get restless and have a longing to explore uncharted lands.'[12] The movies created an ideal of romantic love in which attitudes and techniques were copied from Rudolph Valentino, John Gilbert, Ronald Colman ('the only actor who has ever stirred me to romantic speculations. I think possibly because he was a gentleman') or Theda Bara, Gloria Swanson or Clara Bow.

The industry appreciated the value of these infatuations and built up the image of their stars by 'type casting', by massive press campaigns in the new movie magazines, and by encourag-

Rudolph Valentino: as a young Italian immigrant (above), as a box office star, and laid out in a dinner jacket after his sudden death in August 1926 (opposite)

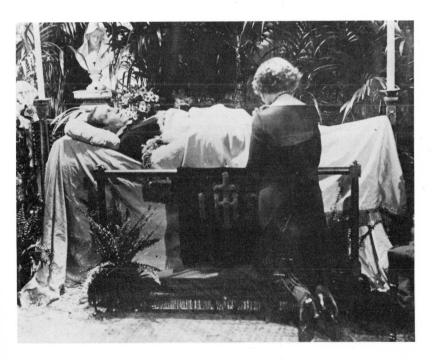

ing the flow of fan mail to Hollywood from all over the Western world. A high proportion of the fan mail came from women, young and middle-aged, single and married. The cinema of the 1920s and 1930s was to a large extent a woman's entertainment, and commercial films were made to please a female audience. The customers were not overwhelmingly female, but women were in the majority and they were very often the decision-makers in this sphere of entertainment. Mothers took the family to the 'pictures', with or without father, and young women were taken to the 'pictures' by young men who hoped that the price of two cinema seats might win them some part of their girls' favours. The big companies carried out very little market research apart from the random experiments of their 'sneak previews' of features to test audience reactions. The great movie 'moguls' decided at their desks what the public wanted. Their decisions were based on a basic assumption that movies must appeal to and excite, but not alarm, the women of America. The cinema became for millions a dream world in which they could escape from the monotony of lives increasingly standardized by the new mass production techniques of industry and the con-

Winners of a British screen test for young actors required to appear in children's matinée film shows

centration of populations into cities. The psychologist C. G. Jung commented that 'the cinema, like the detective story, makes it possible to experience without danger all the excitement, passion and desirousness which must be repressed in a humanitarian ordering of life'.

Many critics suggested that the excitement and passion were not always repressed or sublimated: the cinema, they were certain, could be an incitement to evil and violence. From the earliest days the cinema produced Westerns and crime stories which threatened dangerous consequences. In 1905 the Optical Lantern and Cinematograph Journal reported that three boys who had been caught breaking into a shop said that they had learned how to do it from a cinema show. The judge of the Children's Court in Brussels complained that 'the Children's Judges of the country are unanimously of the opinion that the harmful influence of the cinema on Belgian youth is one of the principal causes of crime among children'.[13] This sentiment was echoed on 3 September 1915 by Mr Alderman Hanson at the London Guildhall Juvenile Court. 'We have had this afternoon three or four cases in which reference has been made to picture palaces and their most pernicious influence on the minds of young children...There is hardly a juvenile court where instances of this sort are not mentioned.'[14] The British National Council of Public Morals noted that juvenile crime increased as the popularity of the cinema increased but was not convinced that the two were necessarily linked. 1917 was the third year of a war which had taken many fathers away from home and mothers into war work, removing the corrective family influences. Some young people who frequented the cinemas committed petty crimes. On the other hand it could be fairly stated that the young people who committed petty crimes came from the classes who normally frequented cinemas. Many witnesses testified to the value of the motion pictures in keeping poorer children off the streets during the dark, cheerless war-time nights. The Rev T. Horne, Rector of Syresham in Hampshire, was even more positive in his praise: 'With regard to the influence of the cinema and of amusements generally on the young life of the nation, I wish to make the point that the splendid heroism, the dauntless courage, the magnificent comradeship and self sacrifice of the lads and young men who passed from the cinema and its influence to the fighting line, give a direct contradiction to the aspersions cast upon the popular and cheap amusements of the people.'[15] (The Rev T. Horne was also Senior Chaplain to the Showman's Guild of Great Britain and Ireland.)

The debate about the influence of films on the behaviour particularly of the young has continued to this day. Although few criminals went unpunished and few rustlers unhung it was alleged that the cinema glamourized crime, violence and sex in a way which no earlier popular entertainment had done. An American study of the links between crime and films quoted a 20-year-old boy sentenced for robbery who justified his crime by explaining: 'When I see a movie that shows snappy clothes, big cars and lots of money, it makes me want to have them too.'[16] Implanting an urge to make money is not the same as implanting an urge to commit crime. Western and, for that matter, Communist society is largely motivated by the urge to make money and to possess the benefits which money can provide. Films did, however, show to millions of men and women a life-style which few of them were likely to achieve except through crime or some surprising good fortune, and such films must have influenced the minds of many viewers.

Moreover, the cinemas were freely open to women and children of all ages. Not only the films but the picture palaces themselves, dark, dangerous and unhealthy, were regarded with suspicion. They very rarely became the recognized haunts of prostitutes like the music halls and burlesque shows – the very darkness made that difficult – but the darkness encouraged unwelcome approaches to women and children in the audience. William Healy, an American jurist, writing about *The Individual Delinquent* in 1915 asserted that 'Moving Picture Theatres are favourite places for the teaching of homosexual practices', and D. Young, in *Motion Pictures: A Study in Legislation*, quoted the prevalence of new phrases such as 'movie masher' and 'knee flirtation' as evidence of the disturbing use to which the proximity of young people in the cinema could be put.[17] An early section in the British National Committee of Public Morals 1917 Report was headed 'The Moral Danger of Darkness'. It concluded that this did exist, although often exaggerated. An exhibitor explained that complaints were sometimes received but 'when investigation is made it is usually found that the alleged misconduct is nothing more than the privileged

manifestation of affection between the sexes'.[18] In this con-
nexion he was 'reminded of a very true and tender remark
once made by Mr Newbould, the chairman of my Association,
on this subject, when he said that such a sight so "far from
deserving censure should...make our hearts glad"'. And
Mr Barnett, Probation Officer and Court Missioner at the
Westminster Police Court, was sure that the darkened cinema
'does more good than the music halls. May I tell you an instance
of a couple which will interest you. They had applied for
separation orders, and I took up their cases. I took them to a
picture show and made them squeeze together as close as they
could, and with the pictures and the appreciation of them a new
understanding came into their lives.'[19] The Report concluded
that cinemas were not morally dangerous and that young people
were seldom molested, but recommended that there should be
better background lighting and more supervision.

Such an important new medium of entertainment could not
for ever remain exempt from official control and supervision.
Several factors combined to invite investigation in the public
interest. The most obvious was the danger of fire, arising from
highly inflammable film, which was often used with defective
equipment before tightly packed audiences. The famous blaze
at the Paris Charity Bazaar in May 1897 when nearly 200 people
were burnt alive, including many distinguished members of
the French aristocracy – such as the Duchess of Alençon, sister
of the Empress of Austria – was blamed on the cinematograph.
This was only one of countless fires started by careless operators.
By 1914 exhibitors in many countries needed a license for their
cinemas or halls and had to conform to recognized standards
of safety and hygiene.

But many critics alleged that the films were morally as well as
physically inflammatory. The first demand for a censorship of
material was lodged against *Dolorita in the Passion Dance* two
weeks after its first public showing in 1896. Such demands,
not always entirely disinterested, continued, since the established groups of the church, the vaudeville managers and saloon
proprietors, threatened by the popularity of the new entertainment, combined self-interest with their moral indignation at
the corrupting influence of the cinematograph. More than ten
years elapsed before any effective action was taken. In 1907
Chicago introduced local censorship and other cities followed

suit. During the next few years public concern was expressed at three unwholesome aspects of moving pictures – the violence and racial hostility aroused by films of boxing matches, particularly by the defeat of the white ex-heavyweight champion James Jeffries by the Negro Jack Johnson; the commercial representation of Biblical themes, prompted by an uproar over *From the Manger to the Cross* in 1912–13; and the exploitation of sexual themes in Scandinavian and American films about the white slave traffic, a subject of prurient indignation at the time and exposed to the public gaze in *The White Slave*, *Traffic in Souls* and *Damaged Goods*. Exhibitors themselves became alarmed that their freedom might be arbitrarily restricted and began to agitate for some recognized censorship to set a seal of respectability on their goods.

Producers were torn between their respect for moral standards and their fear that such purity might lose them business. How much more satisfactory it would be if the industry could agree to remove temptation. Carl Laemmle revealed in *Motion Picture Weekly* in November 1915 that

several weeks ago I published a straight from the shoulder talk entitled 'Which do you want' asking the exhibitors of America whether they preferred clean, wholesome pictures or smutty ones. Instead of discovering that ninety-five per cent favoured clean pictures, I discovered that at least half, and maybe sixty per cent wanted the pictures to be risqué, which is a French way of saying smutty. The whole thing was an eye opener, so totally different from what I expected that I am stumped. The Universal Picture Company does not pose as a guardian of public morals or public taste. For that reason it is quite possible that we may put out a picture that is off colour now and then as a feeler. We have no such picture yet, but it is easy to make them.[20]

Clearly he would prefer a gentleman's agreement not to market such products before the state intervened to forbid them and to control an entertainment so far free from the official surveillance exercized over theatres.

In both Britain and the United States the first steps had been taken in 1909. The first British Cinematograph Films Act was entitled 'An Act to make better provisions for securing safety at Cinematographic and Other Exhibitions' and established statutory safety standards for public showings. But in addition the Act empowered local authorities to initiate their own censorship control. To forestall official action the industry in 1912 founded the British Board of Film Censors which has continued to operate ever since as a non-governmental but generally accepted arbiter of good taste. From the beginning it introduced the classification of 'U' for 'Universal Exhibition' and 'A' for the films which children under the age of sixteen could only see if accompanied by an adult. The first American equivalent of this body, the US National Board of Censorship, exercized by the Peoples' Institute of New York (an adult education and community centre), commanded less respect and was widely regarded as being unduly dominated by the production companies.

Pressure for public control at the state or national level continued, and in 1921 more than one hundred censorship bills were introduced in thirty-seven state legislatures. The campaign was led by a Nonconformist minister, the Reverend Wilbur Fisk Craft, in a crusade 'to rescue the motion pictures from the hands of the Devil and five hundred un-Christian Jews'. At the same time Hollywood was rocked by a series of scandals, reinforcing the belief that the movie colony was a centre of wild drunken parties and loose living. Mary Pickford's divorce from Owen Moore and speedy remarriage to Douglas Fairbanks had tarnished the image of America's most respected stars, but this shock was completely eclipsed by the trial of Fatty Arbuckle, one of the best known comedians, on a charge of the man-slaughter of Virginia Rappe, a young film actress, during an alcoholic orgy in San Francisco. The court eventually acquitted him but public opinion found him guilty. The Mayors of Philadelphia, Los Angeles, Memphis, Chicago, New York, Pittsburgh, Washington and many other cities and townships ordered the withdrawal of all films in which Arbuckle appeared as an actor. He was never officially reinstated by the movie companies, who hoped to divert popular censure by ostracizing him and by playing down the strange death of drug-taking Wallace Reid, a popular leading male actor.

America, which was trying to resist the degeneration of the Jazz Age by passing a Prohibition Act, insisted that the movies should be cleaned up. Hollywood appointed its own custodian of morals, Will Hays, who in 1922 became President of the Motion Picture Producers and Distributors Association at the princely salary of 100,000 dollars a year. Hays, a Republican

Mid-Western politician and former Postmaster-General in President Harding's cabinet, knew how to conciliate and how to persuade the studios to eliminate subjects and treatments that might offend the American matrons who represented the conscience of the nation. The industry, wanting to encourage cinema-going as a family habit, fostered the production of a standardized product – the family film, 'an artistically immature, morally safe, and highly profitable entertainment'.[21] Hays was successful. The Hollywood product was sanitized. George Bernard Shaw complained that artistic vitality had been killed along with the danger of corruption: 'The danger of the cinema is not the danger of immorality, but of morality; people who like myself frequent the cinemas testify to their desolating romantic morality.' The stigma of the early twenties was removed and in 1930 the Hays Code, a strict, puritanical set of rules for behaviour in front of the camera, was adopted. By censoring itself, the industry in both the United States and Britain forestalled the attempt to impose any governmental control.

The goods became more wholesome and the wrappings they were presented in – the cinemas – more colourful and luxurious, to some extent becoming – in line with 20th-century merchandizing – even more important than the contents. On city sites throughout America and Western Europe arose dream palaces in which for a few hours any customer, rich or poor, could indulge his fantasy and enjoy a standard of comfort and opulence unknown in everyday life. Luxury hotels, opera houses, Broadway or West End theatres were closed territories to the average working man or woman, but the picture palace provided a classless entertainment with comparatively little difference in comfort between the cheap seats at the front of the stalls and the most expensive range in the circle, unlike the sharp contrast between the expensive stalls and the primitive, wooden bench seats in the galleries of most theatres. In America the poor immigrants sought excitement and release in the first primitive nickelodeons. Their children, first-generation American citizens, entered their inheritance of the picture palace and for fifteen or twenty-five cents could pretend to be millionaires.

At their most lavish the great movie houses rivalled the major opera houses in size and magnificence. In November 1919 the movie magazine *Photoplay* lauded the wonders of the Capitol in

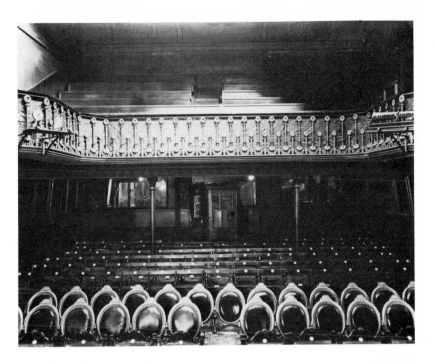

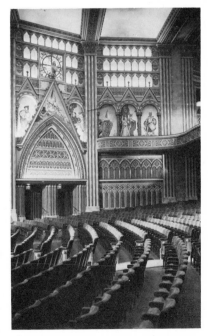

British cinemas develop style: (above) the Egyptian Hall, Piccadilly, pre-1914; (left) the provincial Cinema de Luxe in Walsall, Staffordshire; (right) the Granada, Tooting, with décor inspired by the theatrical designer, Theodore Komisarjevsky

The Astoria cinema in Charing Cross Road, London, epitome of the dream-palace

New York with its 5300 seats and mezzanine floor 'equally suitable for eight-day bicycle races'. The mezzanine, or vast ante-room which wasted space on a scale that would drive a property developer in the 1970s frantic, helped to create the atmosphere of conspicuous consumption. L'Estrange Fawcett wrote that for the great American cinemas

the mezzanine is as essential ... as the film. It is long, about 90 feet or so, built in elaborate style, marbled pillars, decorated arching roof, mirrored walls and cut glass electric chandeliers, enormously thick carpet on the floor, and all round the walls vast divans and luscious arm chairs. There they sit ... as comfortably as if they were in a private suite in the Biltmore or the Ritz Carlton.

It is their club without their even asking for it. They paid their money for the movies and all this wonder was thrown in free.[22]

The service was as exotic as the décor.

At the door more attendants meet them. If the story is a film of Argentine adventure, the ushers are garbed in wide-brimmed beaver hats, black large velvet plus-fours, high boots, coloured neckware and cattle whips. If sheik-business is afoot, they may be Foreign

Legionnaires, and the programme girls may veil their beauty with a yashmak. Thus are Abie and Rosie prepared spiritually for the great adventure they are to undergo in the darkness beyond.

The fantasy was carefully planned. Samuel Katz, manager of one of the major US circuits, explained that 'after the location has been determined, a study of the community is made, a study of the existing theatres, and from that we determine the type of architecture that ought to go with that particular theatre. If the community already has a theatre in the style of the French Renaissance or the Italian Renaissance we will probably take an entirely different type for the architecture of our theatre so as to make it distinctive.'[23] The leading cinema architect, John Eberson, had a range of styles including Andalusian, Egyptian, Persian and Siamese Byzantine. He controlled the firm 'Michelangelo Studios' that produced the decorative plaster work. The greatest impresario in the business was Samuel Rotaphel, 'Roxy', son of a German shoemaker and a Polish mother. He managed most of the prestige houses in New York and ended with his own regular commercial radio show advertising his cinemas. At the height of his fame he opened the greatest cinema of all,

American cinema interior: Loew's Paradise Theatre, designed by John Eberson

the Cathedral of the Motion Picture, the 'Roxy' in New York, built to his specification and bearing his name. His speech at the gala opening concluded: 'Ye portals bright, high and majestic, open to our gaze the path to Wonderland, and show us the realm where fantasy reigns, where romance, where adventure flourish. Let everyday's toil be forgotten under thy sheltering roof – O glorious mighty hall – thy magic and thy charm unite us all to worship at beauty's throne...Let there be light.' After the performance he sighed: 'I'm happy. Take a look at this stupendous theatre. It's the Roxy and I'm Roxy. I'd rather be Roxy than John D. Rockefeller or Henry Ford.'[24]

The Roxy was the ultimate in picture palace luxury. Not all, or even the majority, of cinemas in New York, London, Paris or Madrid had anything like the same grandeur or style. The average cinema-goer in cities, towns and villages throughout the world indulged his fantasy in much more modest surroundings. But thousands of custom-built cinemas were built in areas where theatres or concert halls had been unknown. In most of them an attempt was made to suggest an element of luxury and glamour even if it consisted only of a stucco front and a chandelier-lit foyer attached to a simple brick building with a tin roof. The names themselves were an important part of the make-believe. Even in the Soviet Union as late as 1924 such cinemas survived with opulent bourgeois names and perhaps even suggested the architectural style for the marble grandeur of the Moscow Underground. A British visitor to Petrograd disapproved of

the efforts to improve and perfect the cinema theatre. Externally these palaces are like the classical exhibits in an architectural museum. There is the Parisiana in the Empire style, with its interior resembling the ornate chamber of a palace. There is the Piccadilly in the most approved Greek style, with a circular portico supported by Ionic columns and a frieze of white medallions on a gold ground. Then there is the Soleil with an interior resembling a Roman bath – red and black walls and white reliefs. The Coliseum has an ambitious look. It has a large circular auditorium and was evidently designed on sumptuous lines.[25]

In far distant Harbin, near the borders with China, shows were given in the 'Decadence'.

The impact of the movies on society is difficult to assess

The first British in-flight movie show took place in April 1925

and was inadequately recorded at the time, but they provided the first standardized international public entertainment for the masses. They supplied recreation and release at a time when people moving into towns and cities had more leisure time but inadequate housing and domestic entertainment. In the early stages of the electric and mass consumption age, movies showed standards of dress, furnishing and social behaviour hitherto unknown to millions who had never seen the inside of elegant hotels, restaurants or probably even houses with a bathroom. This was certainly true in America. In Britain and Continental Europe domestic servants were still common into the 1930s. Countless working-class and peasant girls had thus seen high living from 'below stairs' as parlour or kitchen maids. But Hollywood opened a doorway into a dream world inhabited by film stars, most of whom were drawn not from a wealthy aristocracy but from the working class itself. Films were an essential factor in establishing the age of the Common Man.

Movies and politics

The first Edison Vitascope show in April 1896 included *The Monroe Doctrine* and *Cuba Libre,* probably the earliest appearance of political motifs in the cinema. But not until nearly twenty years later in the First World War were the political possibilities of this new medium extensively used. Both the Allied and Central Powers sent cameramen to the front to record war scenes to impress home and neutral audiences. Pro- and anti-intervention films were produced in the United States, and the Western powers despatched film propaganda teams to Petrograd to persuade the Russians to stay in the war. The Bolsheviks later made full political use of their great film talents and prepared the way for the devastating propaganda material of Leni Riefenstahl and other Nazi producers. But the pioneer film-makers were unaware of the political power of their new instrument.

The coronation of Tsar Nicholas II was recorded on film in May 1896 by Doublier and Moisson, two of Lumière's technicians who had worked the projectors at the historic first performances in Paris. A few days after the coronation they set out to photograph the ceremony at which the new Tsar was to distribute gifts to his faithful subjects. To their horror the crowd of nearly half a million panicked, thousands were crushed to death, and the incriminating film of the disaster and the camera itself were confiscated, the earliest example of political censorship. The royal family were intrigued by the new invention. The court photographer, a German called Kurt von Hahn-Jalewski, secured a moving camera and took pictures of official and domestic occasions. The images of Nicholas that were shown in his reign did not always endear him to his subjects. Stephen Graham, an English traveller, described a tour through Russia in 1911 in which he listened to a sailor from the Black Sea Fleet.

What is a sailor's life? Yes, I ask God that question. Last night I was at the dim pictures, the cinematograph, and I saw how all the generals and officers and soldiers stood with their hats off and their heads bowed, saluting the Tsar, and the Tsar alone had his hat on and looked around like a cock on a perch. Good to be the Tsar. Not good to be a sailor.[1]

Nicholas became disenchanted with moving pictures at the end of his life, commenting in 1913: 'I consider cinematography an empty, useless and even pernicious diversion. Only an abnormal person could place this sideshow business on a level with art. It is all nonsense and no importance should be lent to such trash.'[2] His Bolshevik successors used this 'sideshow business' to win mass support for their regime after the Tsar himself had been overthrown.

The Spanish-American War of 1898, fought mainly in Cuba and the Caribbean, was the first to be filmed. The pictures were much less vivid and dramatic than those of the Vietnam War brought into the homes of almost all Americans by television seventy years later, since the equipment used and facilities granted to the cameramen could not compare with the fast film and 'zoom' lenses available to contemporary helicopter-borne television newsreel crews. The war also prompted the first pro-war propaganda films. Like nearly all political comments in the cinema before 1914 they were privately produced and not inspired and sponsored by the government. A movie entitled *Tearing Down the Spanish Flag* showed only the ripping down of an eighteen-inch Spanish emblem and its replacement by the Stars and Stripes, but this was enough to arouse a fervent response from audiences throughout the United States. 'The people went wild,' according to the producer J. Stuart Blackton. Next year they may have gone wilder at the sight of *Raising Old Glory over Morro Castle,* an Edison film in which flags were raised and lowered against the background of a model of the Morro military fort in Cuba. The Spanish-American War was far more popular in America than the Vietnam adventure was to be; the conflict lasted months and not years and was marked by a series of easy but spectacular victories, heralding America's involvement in issues outside her home territory. The fervent audience response to the film was largely accounted for by the popularity of the war, but it hinted at the power of moving pictures to arouse nationalist feeling.

Britain's problems in the Boer War were more complex, and public opinion was by no means unanimous in its support. Pictures of the troops in action in South Africa were brought home, some of them photographed by W. K. L. Dickson, the early associate of Edison. Dickson's book *The Biograph in Battle* recounts his experiences, which included meetings with Winston Churchill at Ladysmith and lunch with Cecil Rhodes at Groot Schuur. Newsreel men were less arrogant than modern television crews, who almost demand that actions be staged or recreated for their benefit. 'Lord Roberts consented to be biographed with all his staff, actually having his table taken out into the sun for the convenience of Mr Dickson.'[3]

During the war crude patriotic features and cartoons appeared on English screens. The style is typified by the Cecil Hepworth production summing up the final outcome, *Peace with Honour* (1902). The catalogue summary reads:

On a marble dais there is a group of British flags guarded by a 'gentle-

Newsreel shot (possibly reconstructed) of troops under fire in the Boer War

man in Khaki' with a big Union Jack. Britannia enters and drawing aside a central flag, discloses a fine portrait of Lord Kitchener, whereat the soldier cheers lustily. Britannia offers up a laurel leaf to Britain's hero and she then leads in a conquered and dispirited Boer. The Briton shakes him heartily by the hand and the Boer, pleased and pacified, sits down beside him on the dais, and smokes the 'pipe of peace' with his late enemy. The picture closes with Britannia smiling on the two – now the firmest of friends. May so end all Great Britain's wars. [4]

These and similar films reflected the patriotic sentiment of the producers and their assessment of public taste, not a calculated effort by political leaders to sell a policy. The Charles Urban Company's film popularizing Britain's new Asiatic ally, *The Home Life of the Jolly Jap,* had no official backing comparable to that which inspired leading articles in *The Times.* The Boer War films were the equivalent of the jingoistic music-hall songs of Disraeli's era rather than the official records produced with great skill and distinction from 1939 to 1945. America, like Britain, approved the Japanese attack on Tsarist Russia's Far Eastern positions: both Anglo-Saxon nations were glad to see the new Asiatic power helping to preserve the 'Open Door' to China, little realizing that thirty years later they would be forced to combine again in common hostility to a far more effective drive into China by the Japanese themselves and forty years later would be pleading for Russian participation in a war against Japan. In 1904 the 'Jolly Jap' was the hero, praised in an American Mutoscope and Biograph film, *The Hero of Liao Yang.* The company could not afford to send a camera team to the battleground but had to make do with actions recreating the incident in Colonel Verbeck's Japanese Garden in the grounds of St John's Military Academy at Maulius, New York.

International affairs provided material for moving pictures from an early stage, but no political party made any sustained effort to exploit the vote-catching powers of the cinema either before 1914 or at any date since then. One of the early exceptions was a very short, twenty-seven-foot movie copyrighted in February 1901. *Terrible Teddy, the Grizzly King* satirized Vice-President Theodore Roosevelt's anxiety to be accepted as a tough frontiersman. He fires a rifle into a tree but brings down only a housecat. Undaunted, he plunges his knife in for the kill and poses for two bystanders, labelled 'My press agent' and

'My photographer'. He finally mounts a horse and rides towards the camera in search of further game.

This satire is an unusual item. There have been few equivalents in the cinema to television's party political broadcasts in Britain or to the party sponsored television broadcasts in America. The official party propaganda films made before the advent of television on a mass scale were usually seen only by the faithful at party meetings and rarely appeared in the commercial cinemas. In the 1930s and 1940s British documentary and Ministry of Information films and the New Deal products of the Roosevelt era in America argued the case for government economic and welfare services, carrying a message favourable to the Labour and Democratic parties respectively, but there has been very little direct party political use of the cinema in Britain. Aldous Huxley and George Orwell warned their readers of the insidious capacity of moving pictures for indoctrination, but without due cause until the coming of television.

The film catalogues for the period 1902–14 reveal examples of the prejudices of directors being translated into private political propaganda. Hepworth's *Alien Invasion* (1905) was one of a series of political pictures. It showed the arrival at London Docks of a steamer crowded with immigrants – Central European Jews rather than Jamaican, Indian or Pakistani labourers. In the words of an early film catalogue: 'The film follows one "invader" taken home by a relative to a tenement room. Twenty other aliens are already crowded into the room. Here they live and eat, their breakfast consisting of the strange viands which are purchasable in the neighbourhood of Petticoat Lane...These are the people who oust the honest British toiler from his work and *this* the manner of their living.'[5] Another Hepworth film entitled *The International Exchange* put the case for tariff reform. In this, John Bull is shut out of overseas markets by high tariffs, but British free trade policy allows foreigners to dump their goods on him at will. At last he decides in favour of FAIR TRADE and shuts his open door, so imported goods now have to pay duty. 'John Bull raises his head, proud, to meet his comrades once more on equal terms. The picture closes with a view of India and Canada linking arms and rejoicing together.'[6] There is no record of any countervailing Free Trade film material, but this did not prevent the Liberals and the Free Trade cause winning a landslide victory in the 1906 General Election.

The Great War was the first large-scale conflict to be fought after most adult males had been given the vote, and governments recognized that their policies must command popular support. If that support did not spontaneously exist, it was necessary to create it. After the outbreak of war, propaganda in speeches, newspapers or the cinema was used for this purpose. Film-makers in the major belligerent nations did not wait for an official directive but immediately produced hastily devised programmes justifying their country's cause and attacking the enemy with pieces such as *The Fatherland Calls, Dead on the Field of Honour, In the Clutches of the Hun.* Even Sarah Bernhardt was pressed into nurse's uniform for *The Mothers of France.*

Regular weekly newsreels had appeared as early as 1908. They had already recorded campaigns in the domestic war waged by the suffragette movements and the confused Balkan Wars of 1912–13. During the summer of 1914 diplomats conferred, armies manoeuvred, battleships steamed across the screens of Europe. The assassination at Sarajevo was not filmed, but the subsequent discussions and mobilizations which converted manoeuvres into battles were extensively covered. Technological improvements meant that many millions of men were to be killed in this war, but the development of photography meant that at least they went to their deaths familiar with the faces and deportment of the Emperors, politicians and generals who drove them to the slaughter.

The first British official cameramen were not sent to the front until late 1915, but the German and French services were operating much earlier. To a later generation, accustomed to the vivid material from the Second World War, the records of action on the Western Front from 1914 to 1918 seem of a very poor quality. They show endless columns of men and horses marching and guns firing, but rarely infantry or tanks under fire. This is partly a result of the restricted size and status of the film units but mostly an inevitable result of the heavy tripod-mounted cameras and slow film used by the cameramen. They could not move with their equipment as easily as the men who advanced with the infantry into the Battle of Alamein. But these early films created a visual link between the soldiers and the audiences at home, helping to strengthen the impression that this was a war in which the whole nation was involved. The effect may be gauged from the evidence given by a boy of

American cameraman in the trenches, 1918

thirteen to the Cinema Commission in 1917. When asked about his favourite programme he replied:

> The best picture I have ever seen was *The Battle of the Ancre and The Advance of the Tanks*. It shows us in old England the privations Tommy has to undergo in blood-sodden France and Belgium. The Tommies went to the trenches stumbling and slipping, but always wore the smile which the Kaiser's legions, try hard as they might, could not brush off. Lords, tinkers, earls, chimney sweeps, side by side, were shown in this splendid film. It showed and proved that although England was small and Germany large, the British Lion was a match for the German Eagle any day. The film also showed that monster terror and fear of the Germans, the Tank. Snorting, creaking, waddling, the huge bogey started for the German front line trenches. The film showed the huge British guns. Day and night, night and day, the huge monsters of destruction roared, never ceasing.[7]

As well as bringing the soldiers to the civilians in France, Britain and America, the cinema brought brief periods of laughter and romance to the troops. Film shows were set up in rest areas behind the lines.

German, French and British war films and propaganda features

War propaganda movie subsidized by the British Government for US consumption. It starred the Gish sisters as victims of brutal Prussians and was directed by Griffith

were sent to neutral nations. They lacked the explosive impact of *Baptism of Fire,* the record of the Nazi invasion of Poland in September 1939 which was distributed to German embassies abroad in the spring of 1940 as a warning to any state seeking to resist Hitler. But they were an essential part of the campaign to win over neutral (and especially American) support with films such as *The German Side of the War, The Log of U-Boat 35,* or *The Kaiser Challenges.* The debate within the United States whether to intervene or remain neutral was reflected in the output of the movie industry. Thomas Ince's *Civilization* was a full-scale attack on the futility of war. It was answered aggressively by Stuart Blackton's *The Battle Cry of Peace,* made in association with Theodore Roosevelt, and by Thomas Dixon's sequel to *The Birth of a Nation* entitled simply *The Fall of a Nation,* which recorded the defeat of pacifist America by an imperialistic European power.

Once war was declared by the United States in April 1917 this debate ended and pacifist films were withdrawn. Studios rushed to film patriotic sagas or anti-German features with names like *The Kaiser, Beast of Berlin* and *The Prussian Cur.*

Lillian Gish and Noel Coward in Griffith's touching war film, Hearts of the World

The Committee on Public Information established a film section whose output included *Pershing's Crusaders,* showing General Pershing's Expeditionary Force in training, and *The American Indian Gets into the War Game.* Films were used for recruiting and military instruction, to raise money for the Red Cross and to sell Liberty Bonds. Chaplin, W. S. Hart and Douglas Fairbanks addressed mass rallies to promote Liberty Bonds. Mary Pickford played in a war film, acting the role of a spy saved at the eleventh hour from a fate worse than death at the hands of her brutal German captors. D. W. Griffith travelled to the front and shot material incorporated in the war melodrama *Hearts of the World.*

The Committee on Public Information used the power of the American film output, which was now far greater and more attractive than that of any other country, to ensure that German film was excluded from the cinemas of the major remaining European neutrals. Sweden, Norway, Holland and Switzerland were informed that no US film would be supplied to any cinema that continued to show German footage. Faced with a choice between the poor-quality German films or the latest adventures of Chaplin or Pickford, neutral exhibitors did not hesitate for long. The material from Berlin vanished from their screens.

The Committee backed this up with a rule that no US entertainment film would be sold to an exhibitor who refused to show an accompanying 20 per cent quota of the Committee's war films. The Allied case was hammered home in the cinemas of the few non-belligerent European nations.

In Britain Sir Max Aitken, M.P. (later Lord Beaverbrook) was quick to appreciate the importance of the camera and encouraged the War Office Cinematographic Committee to send official units to the front. In 1917 Colonel John Buchan, famous as the author of *The Thirty-Nine Steps*, was put in charge of the Department of Information. Films such as *The Battle of the Somme* and *The Advance of the Tanks* were shown at home. Short inspirational messages – 'Save Coal' or 'Buy War Loan' – were included in normal programmes and the mobile cinemas entertained the troops or warned them in *Whatsoever a Man Soweth* of the dangers of venereal disease.

The 1917 February Revolution in Russia and the possibility of a separate Russian peace with Germany alarmed her Western allies. In addition to diplomatic pressure on post-Tsarist governments and the special agents sent to establish contact with the revolutionary parties, propaganda film units were despatched by Britain and America to show the Russian people the power of the Allied war effort. A British party was put under the command of Colonel Bromhead, later to become the Chairman of British Gaumont Pictures, who was given a collection of films showing the British armed forces in action. Bromhead was dissatisfied with this material and would have preferred shots of 'ordinary English public life such as a crowd at an election keeping good order and chaffing with our "bobbies" (who had a great name in Russia), or various scenes relating to the passage of an important Bill'.[8] The unit operated in association with R. Bruce-Lockhart, a British secret agent sent to make contact with the Bolshevik leaders. Lockhart discovered that Bromhead's pessimism was justified.

The effect of these war pictures on the minds of the new undisciplined Russian army can be imagined. Not unnaturally, they seemed merely to increase the number of deserters. It was not Bromhead's fault. He was a splendid fellow, who realized the futility of showing war pictures to men whose sole thought was peace. Still, he had his duty to do.[9]

The American material was equally ineffective. Most of the shipment was stranded in Stockholm. Those films that did arrive appeared in Petrograd after the Bolsheviks, determined to make peace at any price, had taken over power. Edgar Sisson hired a theatre on the Nevski Prospekt and showed his two films *The Presidential Procession* and *Uncle Sam's Immigrant*, retitled *All for Peace through War*. Sisson played down the last words of the title. The feature told the story of an immigrant who makes good in the USA and shows his gratitude by enlisting in the army, together with his American-born son, to fight for his new land. The film aroused little interest and the unit later slipped out of Bolshevik territory to show its material to counter-revolutionary forces in Archangel and Vladivostock.[10] The first attempt to use the cinema as a political weapon had been a complete failure.

A footnote to this story of the Western attempt to pit moving pictures against the oratory of Lenin and the war-weariness of the Russian people is the record of Hollywood's comments on the new Bolshevik regime in feature films produced for home consumption. The 'Red Scare' and American labour unrest frightened Lane, Secretary of the Interior in President Warren Harding's new administration. He summoned motion picture executives to a conference where they pledged themselves to produce stories emphasizing the values of the American way of life and denouncing the evils of Communism. Once again the Reverend Thomas Dixon was on hand to supply suitable material, this time a play called *Comrades* which was filmed as *Bolshevism on Trial* to illustrate 'the impracticability of idealism, the eternal selfishness of human nature' and 'the lunacy of free love'. Other films followed including *The Right to Happiness*, which posed the question: 'Which would you rather have in this country – destruction under the Red Flag or construction and co-operation under the American Flag?'

Similar fears were felt in some quarters in Britain. The National Federation of Discharged and Demobilized Sailors and Soldiers was concerned at the effects of Bolshevik propaganda on ex-service men. The London *Times* reports that the Federation showed a film entitled *Bolshevism; a message of its evils* (most probably one of the American productions) to 200 M.P.s at Westminster in the summer of 1919 and went on to sponsor its showing in fourteen London cinemas in September and subsequently throughout the country. The programme seems to have evoked no enthusiastic response but then neither did the Bolshevik propaganda. As unrest at home subsided and as Soviet Russia ceased to be a revolutionary challenge to the West and instead became a starving country to be pitied and fed by the Hoover Mission, films with overt political messages disappeared from American screens. The Hollywood products of the 1920s were strictly for entertainment.

The Bolsheviks themselves had a major task on hand, that of winning the support of their own peasant population who were more easily reached through pictures than the written word. During the civil war and the early years of consolidation this programme was handicapped by the general lack of cameras, projectors and even film stock. As conditions returned to normal equipment was imported, but it was not until the 1930s that substantial quantities were manufactured at home. In August 1919 all film-making was nationalized. Lenin was clear on the policy to be followed. Programmes should combine a mixture of propaganda and entertainment, 'of course with no indecency or counter-revolution'. The propaganda should include pictures 'from the life of peoples in all countries, contrasting the oppression and misery in the capitalist world – colonial rule in India, starvation in Berlin – with the progress of the new Russia'. Above all they should be spread as widely as possible, especially 'in villages and in the East, where they are yet novelties, and where our propaganda will thus be especially successful'.[11]

Agit-trains carrying books, magazines, teachers, artists and film projectors were organized throughout Soviet territory. *Pravda* reported in 1919: 'During each period when the train was not in motion, the travelling cinema worked with hardly a break, with an ever-changing audience of hundreds of children, local workers and peasants. In the evenings the films were shown on the streets near the train.'[12] Film shows on wheels were not unknown in the West. In March 1924 the London and North Eastern Railway ran cinema coaches on some of its long-distance runs, projecting entertainment rather than propaganda films. The experiment did not last very long and the combination of travel and movies as a commercial idea rarely reappeared until the 'in-flight' movies of the jet aeroplane age. But during the Russian Civil War even an agit-boat with a barge cinema was organized by Molotov and Lenin's wife Krupskaya, and sailed

Cinema as entertainment on board the 'Flying Scotsman' in 1924, and as propaganda on a Soviet agit-train (above and right)

the Kama and Volga rivers. Few suitable films were available but they included the early Soviet newsreels, *Kino Pravda,* produced by Dziga-Vertov, one edition of which shows a mobile cinema with a projector and screen being set up in a city square.

Vertov was one of three remarkable brothers, all of them involved in film-making. Two of them, Dziga and Michael (who kept the family name of Kaufman), stayed in Russia. Boris Kaufman emigrated and worked in France with Jean Vigo on *Zéro de Conduite* and *L'Atalante,* and subsequently in America with Elia Kazan (*On the Waterfront,* 1954) and Sidney Lumet (*Twelve Angry Men,* 1957). Dziga was a leading protagonist of the 'Kino Eye' documentary school, using wherever possible material shot on location often by his cameraman brother Michael. He used few professional actors and shaped his documentary material into fanciful full-length features such as *Man With a Movie Camera* (1929) and *Three Songs of Lenin* (1933).

Within ten years of the October Revolution the Bolsheviks had not only created a widespread cinema network but had produced in Vertov, Eisenstein, Pudovkin and Dovzhenko

The famous Odessa Steps sequence from Battleship Potemkin *(1927)*

some of the greatest masters of the silent cinema. Many of their greatest films were commissioned for a specific political purpose: *Battleship Potemkin* commemorated the tenth anniversary of the mutiny and the 1905 Revolution, while the October 1917 seizure of power prompted the creation of *October* and *The End of St Petersburg*. *The General Line* was part of the programme to encourage the formation of collective farms. Few political regimes have been so successful in sponsoring official art of such outstanding quality. By the time that Russian films achieved recognition in the outside world the early promise of new revolutionary achievements in other arts – literature, drama, architecture and painting – was fading. Experimental work gave way to the conformist line of 'socialist realism' advocated by Stalinists in the late 1920s.

Working in the official cinema was not without its ideological hazards. Eisenstein's *October* was delayed several months by the need to play down the role of Trotsky in the Revolution to correspond with his decline in political favour. (Even though Trotsky was edited out of all Soviet films, the Russians were unable to expunge his chance appearance in a 1914 Vitagraph drama *My Official Wife* shot in New York during Trotsky's sojourn in America as a political refugee.) *The General Line* was revised at Stalin's direct command to take account of changes in the party line on collectivization. He interviewed Eisenstein in the presence of Molotov and Voroshilov and urged him to reconsider the closing reel. 'Life must prompt you to find the correct end for the film. Before going to America, you should travel through the Soviet Union, observe everything, comprehend it and draw your own conclusions about everything you see ...'

'We were sincerely sorry,' records Eisenstein's colleague Alexandrov, 'that the talk with Comrade Stalin had not taken place before we made our film. It would have been a very different film.' Subsequent Soviet history might have been very different history if Stalin had followed his own advice and the other counsel he gave to Eisenstein. 'You should not invent images and events while sitting in your office. You must take them from life – learn from life. Let life teach you!'[13] A year earlier, during the emergency following the 1927 harvest and the poor deliveries of grain by the peasants, the Russian leader had despatched party workers and key members of the polit-bureau to investigate at first hand the problems of the country-side. On 15 January 1928 he travelled himself to Siberia with Molotov, spoke in such centres as Novosobirsk, Rubstovo, Barnaul and Omsk, and for three weeks learnt about the difficulties of Soviet agriculture from life on the farm rather than from party statistical returns. E. H. Carr asserts that 'It was, so far as is known, the only occasion after the death of Lenin on which Stalin undertook a mission to remote rural areas.'[14] The memory of it must have been still fresh in his mind when he recommended a similar tour to Eisenstein and Alexandrov.

Thereafter, in the troubled days of the 1930s drive against the kulaks, with its slaughter of peasants and livestock, Stalin made no further sorties into the countryside. Khruschev in his speech to the Twentieth Communist Party Congress in 1956 declared that

Because Stalin never travelled anywhere, he did not meet city and Kolkhoz workers; he did not know the actual situation in the provinces.

He knew the country and agriculture only from films. And these films had dressed up and beautified the existing situation in agriculture.

Many films so picture Kolkhoz life that the tables were bending from the weight of turkeys and geese. Evidently Stalin thought that it was actually so. [15]

The great Russian silent films became one of the glories of the Communist regime and were its most respected export to the outside world. Western governments were reluctant to sanction their exhibition and they were usually shown only to private cinema clubs. All films coming from Moscow were regarded with suspicion. A ponderous travel film *In Lenin's Land* consigned to the Friends of Soviet Russia was held up by the British customs authorities and eventually awarded a 'U' Certificate by the British Board of Film Censors only under the more acceptable title of *A Journey to Soviet Russia*. Everywhere they excited interest as visual evidence of what was going on in the largely unknown new society in Russia. Some Reichstag deputies seeing the group of warships at the end of *Battleship Potemkin* suspected secret Russian naval construction, unaware that these frames were extracts from old foreign newsreels. The

Enemies of the people – a kulak and his wife from The General Line *(1929)*

more normal reaction was one of artistic admiration and curiosity about a regime that could produce films superior in style and content to even the best achievements of Berlin and Hollywood. Stalin appreciated their value:

The significance of Soviet film art is very great – and not only for us. Abroad there are very few books with Communist content. And our books are seldom known there for they don't read Russian. But they all look at Soviet films with attention and they all understand them. You film-makers can't imagine what responsible work is in your hands. Take serious note of every act, every word of your heroes. Remember that your work will be judged by millions of people.[16]

Fortunately for the Russians their routine output of dreary film dramas and crude propaganda tracts were rarely seen outside their own countŕy. With their greatest films the cinema had reached political maturity, and in Eisenstein's phrase 'became as terrible a weapon as the hand grenade'.[17]

In strong contrast the cinema outside Russia remained for the most part politically a damp squib. In Italy, the only other totalitarian regime of the time, Mussolini never imposed such a tight control on political and cultural life as Stalin did and as Hitler was to achieve. Italy and the Italians enjoyed the show of fascism but suffered comparatively little of the vigorous reality. Traditions and the climate did not favour the creation of effective commissars or gauleiters. But attempts were made to use the cinema to mould public opinion. In 1924 control of films was handed over to L'Unione Cinematographica Educativa (Luce), an official Institute. Two years later all exhibitors were instructed to devote at least ten minutes in each programme to official films sponsored by Luce which expounded party policy on civic affairs, economic development and national culture. Few foreign films, except those admitted on an exchange basis, were shown in Italy in an attempt to protect a weak balance of payments and to insulate the country from the decadent materialism of the American cinema. The results were insignificant. The official films were not regularly available and were of very variable quality. The medium had only a limited importance in a country as poor as Italy in the 1920s, with a predominantly rural population able to support only one third of the number of cinemas in Britain at that time.

The German films of the 1920s conveyed no specific political message and only faint signs of the pre-Nazi nationalist hysteria which some critics claim to identify so clearly. The German company UFA attempted to explain away the German part in the Great War with a film composed of actuality material and vivid maps and diagrams. The result, *Der Weltkrieg*, was as tedious as it was unconvincing. Britain produced comparatively few films in the 1920s and they had few political or other convictions. The French and Scandinavian industries survived by concentrating on comedy and drama without political overtones. Jacques Feyder's *Les Nouveaux Messieurs*, a cynical indictment of the spoils system of the Third Republic, is one of the rare exceptions.

The most important film industry, the American, had no direct political links in the 1920s. President Hoover invited Louis Mayer, President of MGM, to one of his first informal White House lunch parties in 1929 but this was a reward for conventional political support in raising money for the Republican party and not for producing pro-Republican films. William Randolph Hearst, the newspaper millionaire, was passionately involved in both politics and the cinema, but the passions

The dream sequence in the French Senate from Jacques Feyder's banned political satire Les Nouveaux Messieurs *(1929)*

were rarely drawn together. His Hollywood interest was concentrated on the sponsorship of a succession of films for his faithful friend Marion Davies, and in entertaining the leading stars at San Simeon. Films played little part in American politics. Without speech their value was limited, but even in the sound era they have been of little significance. Roosevelt in the 1930s delivered radio 'fireside chats' but no picture palace sermons, and it is doubtful whether the predominantly Republican movie moguls would have allowed him to do so. One Democratic political leader who did make money from films, as we have seen, was Joseph Kennedy. He built up a distributing organization into RKO Radio Pictures in the early days of the talkies, having assessed the competition in 1926 as 'a bunch of pants pressers in Hollywood making themselves millionaires. I could take the whole business away from them.'[18] He made his millions and left as abruptly as he arrived before the economic crash of the thirties.

Although Western films made few direct references to political issues, as an industry the cinema became involved in political action when European film-makers put pressure on their political leaders with the traditional plea from a weak industry for protection against foreign competition. British, French, Italian and German producers lobbied for restrictions on the American films which dominated their home markets and constituted a commercial and cultural challenge. American films stimulated a demand for American goods, motorcars, electrical equipment, consumer goods. Trade no longer followed the flag: it followed the movie, from China to Peru. Dr Klein of the United States Department of Commerce was loud in his praise: 'It is invaluable in China. It is invaluable in all markets where there is a high percentage of illiteracy among the people, for from the pictures they see, they get their impression of how we live, the clothes we wear, and so forth...I can cite you instances of the expansion of trade in the Far East, traceable directly to the effects of the motion picture.'[19] The British Consul in Peru saw how these shows endangered British trade. 'Fashions in behaviour, dress, furniture and houses as seen on the films not merely have an unconscious effect but are sought for. Peruvians with a social problem, a dress to buy, a room to furnish or a house to build will deliberately go to the cinema as to an animated catalogue to get ideas.' He deplored the absence of British animated catalogues.[20]

Chaplin associated more freely with political figures than any other American or British silent film actor or producer. Here he is seen with (left) Max Eastman, an American left-wing intellectual, and (right) Winston Churchill

Chaplin with Amy Johnson (the British aviator), Lady Astor and George Bernard Shaw

In 1923 eighty-five per cent of the films shown in French cinemas were made in America. In November 1924 not a single film was being made in any English studio. The proportion of home-made movies exhibited in British cinemas fell from twenty-five per cent in 1914 to two per cent in 1925. British M.P.s repeatedly expressed concern at the American domination over the minds of cinema audiences, one of them asking in the House of Commons: 'Should we be content if we depended upon foreign literature or upon a foreign press in this country?'[21] A British National Film League was formed in November 1921 to promote home-grown features and to attack the blind- and block-booking of transatlantic material. A luncheon was held on 14 November 1923 attended by the Prince of Wales and five hundred guests to launch a British Film Week. It was easier to provide lunch than an adequate number of films. The Week was not held until the following spring and was succeeded by an even more alarming slump. Politicians and exhibitors in the British Empire, particularly in New Zealand and Australia, bewailed the absence of films from the home country. The complaints were voiced at the Imperial Education Conference in 1923. Mr F. Tate, the Director of Education for Victoria, made clear that

at the outset he would like to register his own opinion that they as British folk ought to view with great concern indeed the fact that millions of people throughout the Empire were daily seeing programmes prepared in foreign countries. The cinematograph, by reason of the fact that it was such a potent instrument in conveying instruction in a very easy and fascinating way, might be made the means of the most insidious propaganda. He was concerned very much with the fact that their people were being familiarized with ways of thinking and acting and speaking that were not British ways.[22]

The Imperial Conference of October 1926 returned to this topic and 'drew attention to the small proportion of films of Empire origin'.

The Times mounted a campaign.

They have called themselves the 'University of the Plain Man', and so by thousands they are regarded. People believe what they see on the screen ... Bad films therefore have the effect of lying teachers, and, to put no fine point on it, their general teaching is opposed to both common sense and Christianity. Their weaker minded devotees become enslaved by a greedy, pseudo-romantic delusion, which is among the psychological causes of our present discontents; the reaction from them is the reaction from deluding drugs.[23]

What *The Times* wanted was better films from all sources; what the politicians produced was a device to encourage the production of British films, hoping that bad British films might be less harmful than bad American films. Their production would at least provide employment for native actors and technicians. In 1927 a Cinematograph Films Act was passed to operate for ten years from January 1928. British exhibitors were to be compelled to show a quota of home-produced films rising from five per cent in 1928 to twenty per cent for 1936–8. For the purpose of the Act a 'British' film was defined as one made by a British subject or a British company in a studio within the British Empire, and from a scenario written by a British subject. At least seventy-five per cent of the salaries and wages must be paid to British subjects. The proposal was attacked in Parliament by the Labour and Liberal Opposition as an abandonment of free trade. Princess Bibesco wrote in *The Times*, 'the British public does not avoid a film because it is British but because it is bad'. One exhibitors' association asserted in phrases reminiscent of the 19th-century free trade advocacy of Cobden and Bright that the Bill 'aims at taking away our constitutional right as British citizens to freely contract and trade in the industry in which we are engaged, and alternatively imposes heavy penalties upon us for exercizing that which hitherto has been our lawful right and the right of every other citizen'. The protest was unsuccessful. The Bill was passed, introducing into this new industry the Protectionism soon to be adopted more generally for a British economy no longer strong enough to maintain the Free Trade principles of the Victorian era. But even this attempt failed, for the big American companies evaded the restriction by sponsoring low-budget movies in British studios ('quota quickies') to comply with the Act and by continuing to pump in their own more expensive and more popular output. Despite the interest of the politicians and the efforts of the Rank Organization in the 1940s and 1950s a strong independent British film industry has never come into existence.

The French and Germans were only slightly more successful. Immediately after the war Germany imposed restrictions on the import of foreign films, as much to preserve its limited stock of gold and foreign currency as to protect its own producers. This was formalized into the 'Contingent' quota decree that for every imported film released, a German film should be produced. By this method output was kept up. From 1923 to 1929 Germany produced an average of 44 per cent of the feature films shown on its screens, compared with 10 per cent in France. The German industry was the third largest in the world, being exceeded only by the United States and Japan. But, as in Britain, many shoddy films were produced merely to satisfy the quota requirement. Again, American agents bought these quota certificates or financed cheap productions to enable them to get licences to import their own more expensive and profitable features.

The rapid expansion of German production attracted speculative money into the industry, including the secret funds of the War Ministry invested by Captain Lohmann in the Phoebus Film Company. When the company went bankrupt in the winter of 1927 not only Lohmann but the War Minister, General Gessler, was forced to resign, giving way to General Gröner, who helped to prepare the path for Hitler's rise to power. In the mid-19th century a scandal surrounding the Scottish-Creole dancer Lola Montez, favourite of the Bavarian King Ludwig I, had precipitated the king's abdication and indirectly opened the gate for the revolutions of 1848. Eighty years later a mistaken investment in the cinema forced a German minister out of office and contributed to the general discrediting of the Weimar Republican era, which persuaded many Germans to welcome the installation of Hitler, a Nazi Chancellor, in 1933.

The French quota was introduced later (1928) and was less ambitious – one native film for every seven imports. A leading newspaper, *Le Matin*, had demanded action for cultural as well as economic reasons: 'The truth is that the Americans are trying to make Europe give way to their ideas and rightly believe that the propaganda in motion pictures which permits the American influence to be placed before the eyes of the public of all countries is the best and least costly method of spreading the national influence.'[24] The Herriot Decree of February 1928 responded to the 'American Challenge' by placing the exhibition of all motion pictures under the control of the Ministry of

Public Instruction and Fine Arts, exercised through a Commission of thirty-two members. Sixteen of these were civil servants, eight were nominated by the industry, and eight were selected to represent informed public opinion. All films, French or foreign, had to obtain a certificate from the Commission, who were instructed to 'take into consideration the whole of the national interest involved, and more particularly the preservation of national customs and traditions, and also in the case of foreign films, the facilities for the release of French films in the countries of origin'.[25] As early as 1910 the Norwegian Parliament had passed a Bill enabling municipalities to own and operate cinemas. By 1921 fifty town and rural municipalities were operating 115 theatres. The profits were used for cultural purposes, creating libraries, art galleries and concert halls. Popular entertainment subsidized more sophisticated arts in the way that the profits on football pools in Continental countries have been used to pay for the provision of sports grounds and indoor halls for non-professional athletes. In 1919 a State Kommunenenes Film Central Company was established to make Norwegian films. Their output, however, was limited and the Norwegian government could only ever hope to control and tax, not replace, American films. Hungary and Italy were other nations that introduced quotas to stem the flood of imports, but no European producers could match the financial resources and professional skills of Hollywood. The arrival of talkies in 1928 momentarily halted the flood until the problems of dubbing and subtitling into other languages were solved.

The European powers were not only concerned with protecting their own industry against American competition, they also became alarmed at the effect of the cinema on their colonial subjects. A *Times* article in September 1926 complained that

the pictures of amorous passion give the Indian a deplorable impression of the morality of the White Man and worse still of the White Woman. The act of kissing, save among the natives who have had the benefits of education, is never practised ... and the prolonged and often erotic exhibition of osculation frequently shown on the screen cannot but arouse in the minds of unsophisticated natives feelings that can better be imagined than described.[26]

Ramsay MacDonald, the first British Socialist Prime Minister, described in the House of Commons how he happened to be wandering up and down in a little village in one of the outposts of civilization ... There I came across a cinema. I was in the company of a very noble and dignified member of the foreign race in whose land I was at the time, and when we passed that cinema it was emblazoned with advertisements which ought to have brought the blush of shame to the cheek of the thickest-skinned and most corrupt and abandoned of men; and the actors in that film were white people ... Certain markets seem almost to be abandoned to that kind of sinful and abominable rubbish, which is held up to those people who, a few years ago, regarded us as being a dominant and ruling people.[27]

The special *Times* Supplement on the Film Industry of 21 February 1922 included an article on the cinema in India deploring the widespread American influence.

When will the Indian Government realize the value of film as propaganda? ... The history of British administration in the past offers material in plenty; our fight against the causes of famine; the wonderful canals and irrigation works constructed all over India by the Public Works Board; life in the isolated frontier posts where the British soldier keeps the invader and marauder at bay. There are many historical instances of loyalty and devotion, and brave heroic acts performed by Gurkha and Sikh. Give the dark face his due! Why not make films of them?[28]

Films, as well as debasing the morals of the young in Europe and seducing them into the American way of life, were also loosening the bonds of Empire. Politicians might have been able to make little use of the cinema, but they were never likely to be able to ignore its influence on the peoples they controlled. The addition of sound to the film image has made it a much more incisive political tool. Television has brought moving pictures of wars, conventions, strikes and debates into the homes of the electorate, and has made these pictures, together with the men who film and edit them, vitally important in determining political behaviour.

CHAPTER SEVEN

Movies become Hollywood

Hollywood's domination of the world's motion picture industry began around 1920 and ended forty years later. Never before or since have a few square miles gained such complete supremacy in the manufacture of a product. Even the distilling of Scotch whisky is scattered over a wider area than Hollywood, a term used to denote the studios of the Los Angeles area, spilling out from Hollywood itself into the San Fernando Valley, Culver City and other suburban lots. At the end of the silent era between 700 and 800 major films a year were produced in this territory, compared with 400 from all the studios of Western Europe and 150 from the Soviet Union. Japan made nearly 500 films a year but they rarely travelled farther afield than India and South-East Asia. Hollywood supplied cinemas throughout the world, making up over eighty per cent of the international trade in films.

Compared with other major industries like iron and steel, textiles, engineering or automobiles, film-making gains little advantage from being near its raw materials or its markets. Both the raw material and the finished product are compact and easily transportable. Film could be cheaply despatched from a small group of Los Angeles studios across the thousands of miles which separated them from the cinemas of Europe or Asia and from the cities of the Eastern United States. Within these studios was concentrated the unique skill of technicians who came originally to use the Californian sunshine for filming and who stayed to enjoy its congenial climate and open society long after most of their work had moved inside to artificially lit studios. To supplement the professional services of the technicians – the camera and lighting crews, the make-up and wardrobe departments, the set designers and continuity girls –

the companies brought in the best European directors and stars. If Hollywood feared the competition of a German director, a Swedish actress or an English script-writer an attractive contract could always be offered to lure them to the American studios. By 1925 movies had become Hollywood, and a high proportion of the world's film-making talent was concentrated there. America, which had adopted European cultural standards in the fields of art, literature and music, also imported Old World talent into the cinema, a field which was to be regarded as distinctively American.

The resulting invasion transformed Southern California, that had once been a remote outpost of the United States reached only by an arduous sea route round Cape Horn, a land and sea route across the waist of Central America or a long wagon trek through the American plains, deserts and mountains. Thousands of men and women rushed to California in the gold rush of 1849: scores of thousands poured in for the movie rush of the 1920s. Reyner Banham's architectural study of Los Angeles has recorded the urban development of this era: 'It brought to Los Angeles an unprecedented and unrepeatable population of genius, neurosis, skill, charlatanry, beauty, vice, talent, and plain old eccentricity, and it brought that population in little over two decades, not the long centuries that most metropolitan cities have required to accumulate a cultured and leisured class.'[1]

The pre-war migration from the cold and darkness of New York or Chicago winters might have ended in the San Francisco Bay area. The climate was nearly as good as Los Angeles and the city was far more attractive and sophisticated with shops, theatres, hotels and a cosmopolitan air totally lacking in the virtually undeveloped Southern Californian port. One of the early groups which travelled west was headed by G. M. Anderson, who acted in films under the name of Broncho Billy, the cowboy hero of Essanay Company. He opened a studio at Niles Canyon across the bay from San Francisco. Later Charlie Chaplin made a few films there but the other companies who moved to the Pacific Coast settled in and around Hollywood, where the sun was more constant and where the Mexican border was less than 150 miles away. The border had its attractions for the independent producers who had left the East Coast to escape the agents of the MPPC and who might need to escape even farther into Mexico to avoid arrest for infringing the Trust's patents.

When they arrived, Hollywood was a small independent township with less than a thousand inhabitants. By 1921 its population had grown to 100,000. The town was not named after any natural feature but called Hollywood by an early settler, Mrs Horace Wilcox, in memory of a friend's summer residence in the Middle West. Southern California was an underdeveloped area. It had missed out on the gold-mining spree of the mid-19th century, which had lured thousands of prospectors to Sacramento and San Francisco in the north. The Los Angeles boom was about to begin in 1910, initially with movies and oil, extending during the Second World War to aircraft production and in the 1960s to space projects, computers and electronics.

The earliest film units appeared in the winter of 1907–8. Two years later D. W. Griffith and his company made films in the West. In 1913 Cecil B. DeMille opened a studio for the Famous Players company on Sunset Boulevard, Hollywood, and made *The Squaw Man*. The barn he used remains part of the Paramount lot today, having been moved when the company left their original home. DeMille, Zukor and their associates had built up Famous Players into the Paramount Corporation and DeMille avowed that he was out to make 'prodigious films with prominent players'. His grandiose mixture of sex and religion created a distinctive Hollywood genre of films from *The Ten Commandments* in 1923, through *The King of Kings* (1927) and *The Sign of the Cross* (1932) to *Samson and Delilah* (1949) and to his second version of *The Ten Commandments* in 1956.

By 1916 fifty per cent of the American output was produced in California, and a few years later its share had risen to over ninety per cent. Studios became larger and more complex. Land was cheap and Carl Laemmle bought up a large estate in San Fernando Valley where – in addition to the studios themselves – he created Universal City with homes, a post office, a private police force and space for location-shooting. Not to be outdone, Thomas Ince established Inceville where he supervised the productions for his company.

The movie-makers settled in. The lavish mansions in Beverly Hills were built for the stars, who began to vie with each other for the possession of the most expensive homes, the largest swimming pool and the most varied fleet of motor cars. The movies brought the era of conspicuous consumption to Los Angeles and preached this gospel to the rest of America and the world at the beginning of the Consumer Age. Hollywood became synonymous with glamour, expensive living and make-believe movies produced to a formula and distributed with ruthless determination. The whole character of the cinema for over thirty years was determined by the accident that the American industry settled in a comparatively primitive Californian city, remote from the mainstream of American political and cultural life. In the 1920s New York and Washington were three days' train journey rather than – as now – a five-hour flight away. This comparative isolation produced a community dominated by the cinema and the fantasy of the cinema, rather than a community in which film directors, writers and stars lived as one professional group intermingled with others. Frank Capra, a leading director of the 1930s, confessed to an interviewer that 'in Hollywood we learn about life only from each other's pictures'. Capra, an immigrant from Sicily, worked with Mack Sennett, directed Harry Langdon comedies and then in the sound era surprised Hollywood by making successful films about unglamorous characters like *Mr Deeds Goes to Town*, *Lady for a Night* and *Meet Mr Doe* (though even these features were marred by the sentimentality and whimsy which appeared all too often when the studios tried to portray humble families).

By the end of the First World War the Hollywood studios were firmly established. Some great films had been produced – *The Birth of a Nation*, *Intolerance*, the Chaplin and Mack Sennett comedies – as well as a vast output of routine material. Directors, actors, technicians were drawn from all parts of the world, establishing high technical standards in the West and ensuring that the remaining film centres found it all the more difficult to compete. In the next decade almost all the best European directors were lured to Hollywood. Some did not remain long, but few were able to resist the opportunity of earning big money and controlling (so they hoped) the production teams of the best equipped studios in the world. Only the Russian cinema remained virtually unpillaged. Eisenstein travelled to America and attempted to make a film there, but was frustrated by tighter controls than he had ever experienced in Moscow. Most of the leading German directors and stars worked in Hollywood. The major German company UFA ran short of capital in the mid-1920s. Paramount and MGM lent it money, but the price was an agreement to sponsor the distribution of American films in Germany and to encourage directors and stars to accept Californian contracts. Ernst Lubitsch, F. W. Murnau, Emil Jannings and Pola Negri abandoned the Berlin Studios. From Scandinavia Victor Sjöstrom and Maurice Stiller were recruited, the latter bringing with him the plump young

F. W. Murnau's first film in Hollywood was Sunrise, *a surprising and impressive mixture of German and American styles. Janet Gaynor and George O'Brien played the backwoods husband and wife*

Victor Sjöstrom (right) directing his last American film, A Lady to Love, *in 1930, a talkie made in both English and German versions and starring Vilma Banky and Edward G. Robinson*

John Gilbert with Greta Garbo in one of her last silent pictures, A Woman of Affairs

Even Greta Garbo had to stoop to pose for publicity stills

The transatlantic film traffic was not all one way. John Barrymore played Sherlock Holmes *in London in 1922*

actress Greta Garbo, who was to become the empress of Hollywood stars in the 1930s. One of her early silent films *The Kiss* was directed by the Belgian Jacques Feyder.

British studios threw up no internationally recognized directors before Alfred Hitchcock, whose career did not start until the end of the silent era and who did not leave for America until the 1940s. But from Britain came actors Herbert Marshall, Clive Brook, Ronald Colman, Basil Rathbone, Cedric Hardwicke and C. Aubrey Smith, who created a stereotype of the aristocratic Englishman which added a further touch of upper-class fantasy to American films, especially after the arrival of 'talkies'. On their transatlantic liners they crossed with the Californian stars imported into England to try to give the ailing British films an injection of star quality – Dorothy Gish, Will Rogers, Tallulah Bankhead, Lionel Barrymore and Anna May Wong. England was regarded above all as the home of great literature and distinguished authors were hired to write scripts or outlines for films at salaries far higher than anything they could command at home. Sir James Barrie, author of *Peter Pan*, Somerset Maugham and Elinor Glyn, whose romantic novels were a

English novelist Elinor Glyn and the 'It Girl', Clara Bow (left)

compelling mixture of mystery, sex and snobbery, were only three of the literary lions bought to provide cultural uplift. The major Hollywood companies, like Renaissance princes, became patrons of the arts. But like William Randolph Hearst who, having bought shiploads of art treasures for his San Simeon estate, left many crates unopened in New York or California, the film moguls had little conception of how to make use of the treasures they had acquired. Possession was an end in itself. Some directors, writers and stars stayed and made a place for themselves in Hollywood. Many left after a short period, but their presence emphasized Hollywood's pre-eminence in the world of the moving picture. René Clair, Abel Gance, Fritz Lang and G. W. Pabst were the only outstanding West European directors of this period who were not tempted to use their skills in Hollywood during the silent era.

The American industry adopted only semi-consciously, and for commercial motives, a policy of monopoly and domination which was outlined for political and racial motives by the Nazis twenty years later. In his diary for 19 May 1942 Göbbels sketches the role he envisaged for the cinema in the New

Hollywood imported European talent and adapted it to Western ways. Maurice Chevalier (right) poses for publicity pictures with the pioneer cowboy star William S. Hart

Economic Order in Europe, as part of the overall plan to subordinate all activity to the needs of the German people.

If the French people on the whole are satisfied with light, cheap stuff, that is the sort of trash we ought to make it our business to produce. It would be lunacy for us to promote competition against ourselves. We must proceed in our film policies as the Americans do in their policies toward the North and South American continents. We must become the dominating cinema power on the European continent. Insofar as pictures are produced in other countries, they must be only of a local or limited character. It must be our aim to prevent, so far as possible, the founding of any new national film industry, and if necessary to engage for Berlin, Vienna or Munich all stars and technicians who might help. [2]

Göbbels' formula remained, like most of the rest of the projected Economic New Order, a dream to be achieved in the thousand-year Reich, but the American supremacy became almost complete until the language problems introduced by sound films and the post-1930 partial collapse of Hollywood enabled native film production to revive in Western Europe.

The talents imported in the 1920s competed with the directors and stars produced by Hollywood itself. Some were European immigrants who had learnt their film techniques in America. Erich von Stroheim, who started by playing Prussian officers in war films and became known as 'the man you love to hate', worked as an assistant director to D. W. Griffith on *Intolerance* and for a period in the 1920s found producers who were rash enough to let him direct films himself. Stroheim had great talent, but he also had a determination to spare neither time nor money in the drive to secure the effects he wanted. Sometimes he got them, but always at immense length; his film *Greed* had to be cut down from forty-two hours to two and a half. By 1930 he was discredited as a director of commercial films and returned to acting in America and France. *Sunset Boulevard*, directed by Billy Wilder in 1950, featured Stroheim in a part that was almost a caricature of his own career. He played the butler to Gloria Swanson in a faded Hollywood manor, the butler a discarded film director and Gloria Swanson a former star, living alone with her fantasies. Another Austrian who learnt his film craft in America and outraged his financial masters was Josef von Sternberg. In the late twenties he produced three movies – *Underworld*, *The Drag Net* and

Erich von Stroheim, Zasu Pitts, and other members of the cast of Stroheim's classic, Greed *(1924)*

Gloria Swanson and Erich von Stroheim parted company over Queen Kelly *in 1928. They were reunited here in* Sunset Boulevard *(1952)*

Thunderbolt – which anticipated the vogue for the tough, realistic gangster films of the 1930s. Ironically he is best remembered for *The Blue Angel*, made in Germany and not in Hollywood. *The Blue Angel* introduced Marlene Dietrich to American audiences. Von Sternberg's first Californian pictures with Dietrich were never as effective as *The Blue Angel* or some of his silent films, which remain among the best achievements of Hollywood in the 1920s.

Outstanding native-born American directors of this period were Cecil B. DeMille, King Vidor, John Ford, Henry King and James Cruze. They produced a variety of films ranging from the early sophisticated comedies of DeMille, *Male and Female* or *Adam's Rib*, through to his later Biblical epics *The Ten Commandments* and *King of Kings*; the strong American dramas of Vidor, *The Big Parade, The Crowd* and King's *Tol'able David* and *Stella Dallas*; to such great outdoor Western epics as Ford's *The Iron Horse* and Cruze's *The Covered Wagon*. They were all professional film-makers, frequently turning out six or more films a year with steady regularity. Sometimes they would produce a film of outstanding merit, but it appeared

A Western saloon scene being filmed for Sam Goldwyn in 1921 on an outdoor studio; a sheet filters the sunlight onto the actors

almost by accident and was submerged among the string of competent but routine works by which they made their money. The average American director worked in a different environment from his Russian, German or French rivals. Eisenstein, Murnau, René Clair made only a fraction of the films expected from an American director to keep up his company's output. As a result they, and also Chaplin, whose financial independence allowed him to make his own films in his own time, could spend an endless amount of time preparing the script, selecting actors and backgrounds, and filming at a comparatively leisurely pace. The American directors' work was organized by the company managers, the great executive producers, who calculated to the last dollar the overheads involved in running the studios for a month, for a day even, and who devised mandatory shooting programmes to ensure that the equipment was fully used at all times. Films followed each other in and out of studios like motorcars on an assembly belt, and this system allowed little scope for artistic experiment and ingenuity.

Considering the nature of the system it is amazing that out of the 700 to 800 feature films produced each year a reasonable number were interesting, enjoyable and fresh, and many can still be appreciated today as examples of the technique of story-telling without the spoken word. Inevitably the European companies produced a higher percentage of films of outstanding quality and pioneered many of the new ideas in film-making and the presentation of picture images. *Battleship Potemkin, The Cabinet of Dr Caligari, The Passion of Joan of Arc, The Last Laugh* are more exciting or moving than any film produced in America in the 1920s. The experimental and surrealist film-makers, Bunuel, Vigó, Salvador Dali, Storck, worked in France or Belgium and there was little American activity comparable to the present-day underground cinema. Robert Flaherty did produce the earliest great documentary film, *Nanook of the North* (1922), for an American fur company and his second study of a primitive people, *Moana*, for Paramount, but rarely could a Hollywood studio sponsor a work that was unlikely to show a profit and certain to appeal only to an intellectual minority.

The best formula for selling pictures was to be able to offer the public a star whom they could admire and with whom

they could identify themselves. The 1920s are the era of the
great silent stars whose publicity and presentation was much
more professionally handled than that of the early box-office
favourites. Chaplin, Mary Pickford and Douglas Fairbanks
lasted throughout the decade. Chaplin, who freed himself from
company contracts in 1922, made only a few films for which
he spent years preparing the script, shooting and cutting. He
was no longer the universal idol of young and old that he had
been during the First World War. He was too remote and already
too controversial a figure because of his outspoken political
views and his irregular sexual life. But despite the remoteness
and controversy, *The Kid, The Circus, The Gold Rush* and *City
Lights* were eagerly acclaimed throughout the world.

Fairbanks and Pickford occupied a different place in people's
affections. Mary was still immensely popular and produced a
steady stream of successful films. She remained 'America's
Sweetheart' but the sweetheart of the middle-aged and elderly
rather than of the young, who preferred the more direct sex
appeal of Pola Negri, Gloria Swanson or Clara Bow. Her husband
Douglas Fairbanks starred in more grandiose productions
designed to show off his torso and his athletic prowess. *The
Three Musketeers, Robin Hood, The Thief of Baghdad* presented
this all-American college football hero in a variety of costumes
and adventures in which he appealed to old and young, male
and female. Above all he was active; for him 'the world was
not a stage, it was a gymnasium'.[3] Fairbanks was occasionally
mischievous and ruthless, but he was always chivalrous and
honest. He created an image of the forceful upright hero which
dispelled many of the doubts surrounding the moral rectitude
of Hollywood stars at the time of the Arbuckle scandal. Even
the shocking speed of his marriage to Mary Pickford was
forgotten and Douglas was looked up to as a pillar of society.
This position was recognized by the Boy Scouts of America,
who encouraged him to publish in 1924 a book of advice for
boys called *Youth Points the Way*. Fairbanks drew on his own
experiences to propound the recipe for a healthy and successful
life. The book reads like an elongated School Prize Day address,
with chapters headed 'Enthusiasm and Obstacles', 'The Only
Medicine I Ever Take', 'Sunrise and Other Things', 'On Getting
a Start in Life', 'The Other Fellow's Point of View' and 'Keep
on Moving'. The philosophy was the simple, optimistic,

Hollywood (Douglas Fairbanks and Josef von Sternberg, right) with Babe Ruth (left), the baseball king, and a fellow-player

Douglas Fairbanks and director Albert Parker rehearsing for The Black Pirate *(1926)*

Mary Pickford at the height of her fame in Tess of the Storm Country *(1922) with Lloyd Hughes*

confident philosophy of the Coolidge era before the Great Depression, the Second World War, Soviet strength, racial and ecological problems undermined the happy confidence nourished by the Californian sunshine. Mary and Douglas radiated this happy, wholesome confidence. For fifteen years they lived together in their home 'Pickfair', the accepted social leaders of the film colony, entertaining visiting royalty as though they were royalty themselves. Strangely enough they did not appear together in a major film until the talkie *The Taming of the Shrew* in 1930, completed as their marriage was breaking up.

These three great figures had escaped the control of the companies by winning enough fame and money to make their own films for United Artists. Buster Keaton and Harold Lloyd were the only other two stars able to do this. The rest were tied by contracts to the companies who made them and who built them up as assets to be used in ensuring box-office success. Their names and pictures were plastered over billboards and pushed into the columns of the film fans' magazines. Details of their real or imaginary love life were fed to gossip writers. Their followers were encouraged to envy them for their glamorous, opulent existence, but lest this should alienate sympathy they were constantly reminded of the hard life which film work entailed – early morning calls, hours spent in the make-up rooms, the risks and discomforts in shooting many films. One movie magazine assured its readers that 'in Hollywood, health, friends, beauty, even life itself are sacrificed on the terrible altar of ambition...notwithstanding the splendours of stardom, the stars themselves assure you that you wouldn't really like it. It is too tough.'

The public relations techniques which are now an accepted part of the political business world, as well as of the entertainment industry, were created to project the film stars of the 1920s. Paul Mayersberg in *Hollywood, the Haunted House* asserts that 'although stardom is a concept that now applies to a best-selling novel, or a pop group, or a racing driver, it was initiated by the movies...The star is Hollywood's gift to the twentieth century.'[4] This is under-estimating the appeal of 19th-century theatrical, operatic or music-hall 'stars', from Jenny Lind to Marie Lloyd, but even they were not widely known or so systematically promoted as Greta Garbo or Pola Negri.

By the end of the silent era movies had become synonymous with Hollywood. Any danger of competition from the German industry, the only one which possessed anything like the studio resources of Southern California, had been avoided. American companies held substantial interests in the production and distribution agencies of Western Europe, the British Commonwealth and Latin America, their major markets. The small township of Hollywood had achieved a fame more widely spread than that of Athens, Rome or Florence. Thousands of movie-struck men and women travelled there every year hoping that they would be discovered and launched into stardom. Millions of letters poured into the studio post-rooms each week. The moving-picture machine pioneered by Frenchmen, Americans, Englishmen and Germans acquired an unmistakably Californian viewpoint. They were soon to acquire an unmistakably American accent and start the process by which English (even if American in style) has become the most widely used international language since the end of the common use of medieval Latin.

CHAPTER
EIGHT

Pictures move and
talk

The first talking picture was *The Jazz Singer*, shown in New York on 6 October 1927. Appropriately enough for an industry dominated by Jewish producers, it told the story of a Jewish singer (Al Jolson) torn between his loyalty to his family background and his ambition to make good on Broadway. Despite this unpromising theme and a treatment that included several scenes of a synagogue service, the film was a great success and restored the sliding fortunes of Warner Brothers. The public queued up to see and hear Al Jolson singing and even speaking a few words of dialogue. 'Hear Jolson's Golden Voice on the Silver Screen.' *The Jazz Singer* was not the first sound picture nor was it the first all-talking picture. It had almost as many written titles as a normal silent, but it was the first feature film with musical sound and some spoken dialogue, and goes down in history as the first 'talkie'.

Attempts to synchronize sound with moving pictures are as old as the medium itself. Edison's major interest had been in his efforts to combine the Kinetoscope pictures with his other invention, the phonograph. But neither Edison nor the many other pioneers who experimented with a combination of cinematograph and gramophone was able to solve the problem of combining sound and movement on the screen. A subsidiary problem with early equipment was the limited volume that could be produced from early gramophones until the development of radio valves enabled the sound to be easily amplified. This was solved with the development of broadcasting equipment, creating first the sound radio (a serious competitor of the cinema in the early 1920s) and then the talking film, which enabled the cinema to hold off its rival until television appeared, combining the visual appeal of the cinema with radio's flexible entry into the homes of its patrons.

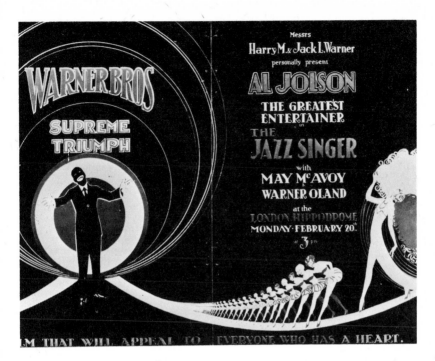

The Jazz Singer *comes to London*

The first completely successful synchronized sound cinematographic equipment was perfected by the Western Electric Division of Bell Telephone Company. The Company linked up with the Warner Brothers Film Company. The four Warner brothers, Harry, Jack, Samuel and Albert, had travelled from Poland with their family to the USA and started their commercial career running a bicycle repair shop. In 1903 they began to exhibit films and built up a distributing and eventually a producing company. But in the mid-twenties they were overshadowed by the giants of the industry – Paramount, MGM, Fox, First National, Universal and United Artists. Their major assets were the stars Irene Rich and John Barrymore and the Alsatian dog Rin-Tin-Tin, whose film exploits produced a steady return for Warner Brothers and for his owner, ex-Sergeant Lee Duncan. The dog had been abandoned by the German army in France in 1918 and brought back to America by Sergeant Duncan. This cleverly trained animal made twenty-two adventure films and was rewarded with a five-roomed kennel in his master's estate in Beverly Hills. Five generations of Rin-Tin-Tins maintained the canine succession into the

Rin-Tin-Tin with his master, Sergeant Lee Duncan (left)

television era. But two stars and a dog did not compensate Warner Brothers for the lack of a chain of first-run cinemas. In 1923 they produced only eleven feature films compared with over sixty each by Paramount, Universal and the companies making up MGM. But with the advent of sound their lack of theatres proved to be an advantage – they were more prepared to experiment with the new apparatus since they would not also have to find the capital to install sound equipment in a big chain of cinemas.

In 1926 they invested 800,000 dollars in the Western Electric equipment, patented as Vitaphone, and began to produce the first films with a sound accompaniment, recorded not on the margin of the film as with later stock but on discs which could be synchronized with the screen images. At first Warner Brothers were not sure how to use their new invention. Sam Warner pointed out that it would enable actors to speak. 'Who the hell wants to hear actors talk?' Harry argued. 'The music – that's the big plus about this.'[1]

The first efforts were one- and two-reel comedies, followed by a full length *Don Juan* starring John Barrymore. The film had a synchronized musical score played by the New York Philharmonic Orchestra and sung by the Metropolitan Opera Company chorus, but no speech. The Fox Company followed Warner Brothers into this field and bought the American rights for a German system they called Movietone and which was used for Fox-Movietone newsreels, including the historic presentation by President Coolidge of a Congressional Medal to Charles Lindbergh, the first man to make a solo flight across the Atlantic.

Warner Brothers, however, were the first to produce a complete feature film backed with sound, including the singing and speaking voices of some of the characters. *The Jazz Singer* featured Al Jolson, for many years a successful vaudeville artist but ineffective on the screen until his voice could be heard. The story of the film paralleled some features of Jolson's own life. He had been born in St Petersburg, Russia, becoming yet another of the East European immigrants moving into America and eventually the movie business. Jolson, like his screen Jazz Singer, left his orthodox family and role as cantor in the synagogue to perform in the music halls. The film was an outstanding success, and the competition from radio was defeated. A second Jolson picture, *The Singing Fool*, appeared. *The Lights of New York* was the first full-length talking picture. For eighteen months after the appearance of *The Jazz Singer* cinemas in America showed both sound and silent films as studios and picture palaces converted to the new system. Features which started as silents were changed over to sound during their production. New equipment, and the money to buy the equipment, had to be found. In Europe the transition was much slower. *The Jazz Singer* was not shown even in London until nearly a year after its New York premiere.

By 1929 the changeover was largely completed in the major American towns. In that year Hollywood produced 395 sound films and 175 silents, almost all low-budget films. By the end of the year the number of American cinemas equipped to show sound films had grown to 8741 compared with 157 in January 1928. 10,000 remained unconverted but they were the smaller halls. Audiences grew rapidly. Total attendances averaged under 60 million a week in 1927, over 90 million in 1930. Profits rose with them. Warner Brothers, who had shown losses in 1925, 1926 and 1927, recorded profits of over two million dollars in 1928 and of 17 million dollars in 1929, enjoying their share of royalty payments for the Western Electric equipment as well as the proceeds from their films. In 1929 they were able to take over First National, the company formed to challenge Paramount ten years earlier, and they became one of the major companies, with a chain of American and European movie houses. From midsummer 1928 the other companies converted to sound and their business also improved. Paramount's profits nearly doubled from 8·7 million dollars in 1928 to 15·5 million in 1929. The industry was rescued from the doldrums of the mid-twenties when over-investment in prestige cinemas had produced losses. 1929 became a boom year with profits that were not to be matched until the 1940s. Not only profits rose in 1929 but seat prices also. The average cost was now 45 to 50 cents, a far cry from the nickelodeon. The arrival of sound enabled the film industry to swim against the economic tide, for a brief period at least. The Great Depression which started with the New York Stock Market collapse in October 1929 did not hit Hollywood for another twelve or eighteen months.

Sound affected more than the finances of the industry: it revolutionized the whole process of film-making. Kevin Brownlow asserts that 'Instead of a gentle grafting, the arrival of sound acted as a brutal transplanting; the cinema was ripped out of the silent era by the roots, and transplanted into a new soil – richer but unfamiliar. Unable to adjust to the new conditions, some of the roots withered and died, and much strength was lost.'[2] For a period it seemed as if the artistic standards of the best silent film-makers might be lost or prejudiced.

Sound equipment restricted, almost as much as it expanded, the scope of the film-maker. Admittedly dialogue could now clarify in a few words situations that needed several sequences of pictures to explain. Sound swept away the intrusive subtitles that slowed down action and were an affront to the whole conception of a moving picture medium. Far more complex ideas and emotions could be expressed by the spoken word than by mime alone. But there were also disadvantages, especially in the years of the earliest equipment. The microphones picked up all noise, including that of the camera itself. This had to be enclosed in a soundproof booth and lost the mobility

MGM converting their lion to sound

it had gained during the preceding fifteen years. It was almost as though the cinema was back to the early days of static shooting of actors performing on a small, severely circumscribed stage. Directors could no longer shout instructions to the actors and extras as the cameras were turning. Scenes needed to be more carefully rehearsed and then shot with no background noise. Off-stage music could not be used to induce the appropriate mood. Betty Compson would have to cry without the aid of 'Mighty Like a Rose'. Actors and actresses would be chosen for their capacity to speak as well as emote in the studios. Silent stars had to change their skills and adopt the methods of the stage actor or give way to performers trained in the theatre. This reversed the events of the pre-war period when stage actors had to abandon their rhetoric and slow extravagant gestures if they hoped to succeed in the new motion picture medium; now film stars had to learn to speak.

Some stars disappeared almost immediately since their voices did not match their appearance. Others went into decline and lost their appeal. Mary Pickford and Douglas Fairbanks ceased to rule Hollywood, but it is difficult to tell whether their demise was a result of the coming of sound or whether it would have come in any case. By 1930 Douglas was forty-seven and Mary only ten years younger. Even celluloid sweethearts cannot last forever. Many foreign artists were unable to perform adequately in an alien language: Pola Negri, Conrad Veidt and Emil Jannings returned to Europe, the latter to make his greatest success, *The Blue Angel,* with Marlene Dietrich. Greta Garbo, about whose voice the greatest doubts were expressed, triumphed. Her throaty Scandinavian intonation made her even more intriguing and imperious.

New script-writers had to be found who could write dialogue as well as invent or adapt stories for film purposes. Hollywood turned to the most obvious source and bought up playwrights and their stage plays. For thousands of cinema musicians the new development spelt disaster. They were now replaced by a musical sound track and thrown out of work at the very moment when the depression made it almost impossible to find alternative employment. Live music in the picture palaces was left to the cinema organists. The amplified Wurlitzer organs appeared just before the talkies and were intended to provide a variety of sounds for one-man musical accompaniments. These were now redundant and the cinema organ flourished in the 1930s as a solo feature in its own right, caressed by ingratiating moustachioed executants playing 'Bells Across the Meadow' or 'Ave Maria' in a soft spotlight.

Few critics welcomed the 'talkies'. F. E. Adams predicted that 'Talkies are merely a temporary craze, like broadcasting and greyhound racing',[3] a strange comment in 1929 when radio was already seven years old. Ernest Betts wrote in *Heraclitus: The Future of Films*: 'The film of a hundred years hence, if it is true to itself, will still be silent but it will be saying more than ever.'[4] His book was overtaken by events and in an addendum to the published work he hurled defiance:

Since the above was written speaking films have been launched as a commercial proposition, as the general pattern of the film of the future. As a matter of fact their acceptance marks the most spectacular act of self-destruction that has yet come out of Hollywood, and violates the film's proper function at its source. The soul of the film – its eloquent and vital silence – is destroyed. The film now returns to the circus, whence it came, among the freaks, and fat ladies.[5]

Alfred Hitchcock directing German actress Anny Ondra in his first sound production,
Blackmail *(1929), with the camera behind a glass screen. Most of the film had to be
re-shot to cater for the recent arrival of sound*

*Hitchcock in one of the miniature roles he so enjoyed, from the same film. John Longdon
and Anny Ondra star*

Despite these gloomy predictions the art of the cinema survived. New techniques had to be created and mastered. For a brief period the cinema was driven back into the theatre. The novelty of speech and the restriction of movement for both the actors and the camera produced a sequence of filmed plays or musical shows. But soon new methods were created as directors realized that sound meant more than just talk. Other noises could be recorded and used dramatically. The custard-pie, slapstick comedy disappeared. It was already dying in the mid-twenties and a more sophisticated silent comedy of mime and characterization had followed it. But Buster Keaton, the master of this style, was unable to come to terms with sound or, alas, for a time with his own personality and problems. Harold Lloyd's skills could be more easily modified, although his greatest era ended in 1930. Chaplin refused to compromise his pantomime with dialogue. 'Talking', he was alleged to have explained, 'will not heighten illusion but destroy it. Films need dialogue about as much as Beethoven's Symphonies need lyrics.' Chaplin was rich enough and talented enough to defy sound and to produce more silent comedies or comedies with a musical but speechless sound track, such as *City Lights* in 1931 or even, in 1936, *Modern Times*. Laurel and Hardy improved with sound, and a new style of humour was born with the Marx Brothers, whose talents included the spoken wit of Groucho and the dumb play of Harpo, a mixture of both sound and silent comedy.

Initially sound films were made more quickly. Microphones could only be used easily indoors, so features were predominantly shot inside the studios with little or no time-consuming location work. The use of speech slowed down the rhythm of films and enabled them to be made with fewer, longer sequences. The average silent feature had been made in eight to ten weeks in 1926–7. The first sound films could be produced sometimes in two. Talkies had longer runs, so fewer films were needed to fill the picture houses. This made bigger profits for the companies but provided less work for the players and the technical staff. A new salary and wage structure had to be worked out at a time when the Depression was throwing millions of Americans out of work. The transition was painful but unavoidable.

It was even more alarming for the Soviet industry. Russian producers had only recently overcome the shortage of raw film stock. Russia's limited financial and technical resources made it difficult for them to change over to sound films. Once again Soviet directors had spare time to indulge in theorizing about the technical problems of the cinema. In August 1928 Eisenstein and Pudovkin issued a joint statement on the implications of sound for their art. They recognized its importance and admitted that Russia would be slow to introduce it into studios and theatres. But they puritanically insisted that it should not be used only as a novelty – 'along the line of satisfying simple curiosity'.[6] In some unspecified way it should be used to increase montage and should include non-synchronized sound to produce an orchestral counterpoint of visual and aural images. Behind this obscure lament lay the realization of Soviet film-makers and their masters that movies with Russian dialogue would be even more difficult to market than films with English- or French-spoken dialogue. The Soviet Union could be spoken of as the 'Socialist Sixth of the World' but very few people in the remaining five-sixths could speak or understand Russian. Eisenstein, with several colleagues, left the Soviet Union to study sound techniques in Hollywood and to indulge in his own abortive attempts at directing a film in the West. Sound came only slowly to the Soviet cinema, and its technical problems, together with the ideological convulsions of the 1930s, ended the period of Russian leadership in the art of the film.

Sam Warner had died on the eve of the showing of *The Jazz Singer*, which was to make the fortune of his company. With it was dying the whole era of the silent moving pictures as well. The movies had been born, and now the infant industry was talking and singing to the world. The cinema lost some of its original quality and beauty when it added sound to its pictures. Fortunately although the silent cinema is dead its spirit lives on. Silent films have been preserved in archives and private collections. They can be seen projected at full scale in revivals at commercial or specialist cinemas. 16- and 8-millimetre copies of many of the major films are available and can be hired for showing by film clubs or in the home. Silent films are sometimes shown on television, unfortunately all too often in extracts moulded into a 'special presentation', accompanied by a patronizing commentary and inappropriate music. But it is possible to see again and marvel at some of the greatest achievements of the early cinema. *The Birth of a Nation* and *Battleship*

Potemkin remain as exciting as ever. Von Stroheim's *Greed* or Murnau's *The Last Laugh* still portray the collapse of a human personality as tragically as any novel or play. The comedy of Chaplin, Keaton or Harry Langdon has no counterpart in any other medium. They can all be seen, studied and enjoyed for their own sakes. They are also of great interest to the historian of literature, society, politics, industry and public opinion. The silent films from 1895 to 1927 recreate for us the society which created them.

The art of the silent cinema is different from that of the theatre, the talking picture or television, and still holds its own place. Yet while we can see some – not alas all or even a substantial proportion – of the thousands of films produced from 1895 to 1930, we can never recapture the impact they made at their first showings. Generations have grown up which have taken for granted the talkies, cinerama, coloured films and television. Silent films now look as technically archaic as vintage motorcars or early locomotives. But many of them have the beauty and integrity of these early machines and they have in addition the quality imported by the great artists – Griffith, Eisenstein, Chaplin, Stiller and others – who chose to express their ideas in this medium. The passage of time does not diminish the quality of good painting, music and literature. It should not diminish the quality of good silent films – a minor form of art – provided that we can preserve some of the freshness of their images and provided that the viewers recall the limitations under which they were made and the nature of the popular audiences for whom they were devised.

REFERENCES

CHAPTER ONE

1 George Pearson, *Flashback*, London: Allen and Unwin, 1957, p. 14.
2 C. W. Ceram, *The Archaeology of the Cinema*, London: Thames and Hudson, 1965, pp. 157 and 201.
3 S. Kracauer, *Nature of Film*, London: Dennis Dobson, 1961, p. 31.
4 Jay Leyda, *Kino*, London: Allen and Unwin, 1960, p. 407.
5 Leon Edel, *Henry James. The Treacherous Years 1895–1900*, London: Rupert Hart-Davis, 1969, p. 166.
6 Rachael Low and Roger Manvell, *The History of the British Film, 1896–1906*, London: Allen and Unwin, 1948, p. 53.
7 M. Bardèche and R. Brasillach, translated by Iris Barry, *History of the Film*, London: Allen and Unwin, 1938, p. 10.
8 Philip French, *The Movie Moguls*, London: Weidenfeld and Nicolson, 1969, p. 28.
9 Lewis Jacobs, *The Rise of the American Film*, New York: Harcourt Brace, 1939, p. 61.
10 E. Wagenknecht, *Movies in the Age of Innocence*, Norman: University of Oklahoma Press, 1962, p. 62.
11 *ibid.*, p. 142.
12 King Vidor, *A Tree is a Tree*, London: Longmans Green, 1954, p. 37.
13 G. Pearson, *op. cit.*, p. 29.

CHAPTER TWO

1 R. S. Randall, *Censorship of the Movies*, Madison: University of Wisconsin Press, 1968, p. 3.
2 M. Bardèche and R. Brasillach, *op. cit.*, p. 46.
3 C. Hoffman, *Sound for Silents*, New York: D.B.S. Publications, 1970.
4 J. Leyda, *op. cit.*, p. 189.
5 Ernest Betts, *Heraclitus: The Future of Films*, London: Kegan Paul, 1928, p. 63.
6 Ivor Montagu, *Film World*, London: Penguin Books, 1964, p. 59.

7   Adrian Brunel, *Nice Work*, London: Forbes Robertson, 1949, p. 15.

8   S. Kracauer, *op. cit.*, p. 94.

9   Hilary Bell, *New York Herald*, 3 December 1899.

10 James Agee, *Agee on Film*, London: Peter Owen, 1941, Volume I, p. 397.

11 Linda Arvidson, *When the Movies Were Young*, New York: Dover Publications, 1969, p. 66.

12 H. Geduld, *Focus on D. W. Griffith*, Englewood Cliffs, New Jersey: Prentice Hall, 1971, p. 52.

13 J. Leyda, *Sewanee Review*, 1949.

14 A. N. Vardac, *Stage to Screen*, Cambridge: Harvard University Press, 1949, p. 64.

15 H. Geduld, *op. cit.*, p. 102.

16 *The Times* Film Supplement, 21 February 1922.

17 H. Geduld, *op. cit.*, p. 98.

18 D. W. Griffith, *The Rise and Fall of Free Speech in America*, Los Angeles, 1916.

19 Alexander Walker, *Stardom*, London: Michael Joseph, 1970, p. 97.

20 D. Robinson, *Buster Keaton*, London: Secker and Warburg, 1969, p. 179.

CHAPTER THREE

1   Rachael Low, *The History of the British Film 1918–29*, London: George Allen and Unwin, 1971, p. 271.

2   S. Eisenstein, *The Film Sense*, translated by J. Leyda, London: Faber and Faber, 1948, p. 14.

3   G. C. Pratt, *Spellbound in Darkness*, Rochester: University Press, 1966, p. 364.

4   Ivor Montagu, *With Eisenstein in Hollywood*, Berlin: Seven Seas Publishers, 1968, p. 122.

5   P. Wollen, *Signs and Meanings in the Cinema*, London: Secker and Warburg, 1969, p. 15.

6   *The Film in National Life*: The Report of the Commission on Educational and Cultural Films, London: Allen and Unwin, 1932, p. 10.

7   Michael Balcon presents *A Lifetime of Films*, London: Hutchinson, 1969, p. 36.

CHAPTER FOUR

1   J. P. Kennedy, *The Story of the Films*, Chicago: A. W. Shaw, 1927, p. 190.

2   Jesse Lasky with Don Weldon, *I Blow My Own Horn*, London: Victor Gollancz, 1957, p. 197.

3   'In the Matter of Famous Players-Lasky Corporation', Federal Trade Commission Decisions, Volume XI, 1928, p. 193.

4 R. J. Whalen, *The Founding Father. The Story of Joseph P. Kennedy*, New York: New American Library, 1964, p. 79.
5 Federal Trade Commission Decisions 1928, *op. cit.*, p. 188. (See also Ralph Cassidy, Jr. 'Impact of the Paramount Decision on Motion Picture Distribution and Price Making', Southern California Law Review, Volume 31.)
6 R. J. Whalen, *op. cit.*, p. 95.

CHAPTER FIVE

1 J. Leyda, *op. cit.*, p. 82.
2 E. Wagenknecht, *op. cit.*, p. 8.
3 J. Leyda, *op. cit.*, p. 161.
4 René Jeanne and Charles Ford, *Histoire Encyclopédique du Cinéma*, Volume II, Paris: Laffont, 1952, p. 276.
5 *The Cinema: Its Present Position and Future Possibilities*, London: Williams and Norgate, 1917, p. xvii.
6 *ibid.*, p. lxviii.
7 A. Marwick, *Britain in the Century of Total War*, London: Bodley Head, 1968, p. 186.
8 S. Rowson, 'A Statistical Survey of the Cinema Industry in Great Britain in 1934'. Journal of the Royal Statistical Society, 1936, pp. 67–119.
9 Compton Mackenzie, *My Life and Times, Octave Five, 1915–23*, London: Chatto and Windus, 1966, p. 193.
10 J. P. Mayer, *British Cinemas and their Audiences*, London: Dobson and Dobson, 1948, p. 16.
11 *ibid.*, p. 32.
12 *ibid.*, p. 53.
13 W. Seabury, *Motion Picture Problems*, New York: Avondale Press, 1929, p. 31.
14 *The Times*, 4 September 1915.
15 *The Cinema: Its Present Position and Future Possibilities*, *op. cit.*, p. 184.
16 H. Blumer and P. M. Hauser, *Movies, Delinquency and Crime*, New York: Macmillan, 1933, p. 45.
17 William Healy, *The Individual Delinquent*, London: Macmillan, 1913, and D. Y. Young, *Motion Pictures, A Study in Social Legislation*, Philadelphia: Westbrook Publishing Co., 1922, p. 6.
18 *The Cinema: Its Present Position and Future Possibilities*, *op. cit.*, p. 83.
19 *ibid.*, p. 208.
20 Carl Laemmle, *Motion Picture Weekly*, November 1915.
21 R. S. Randall, *op. cit.*, p. 9.
22 L'Estrange Fawcett, *Films: Facts and Forecasts*, London: Geoffrey Bles, 1927, p. 80.

23 J. P. Kennedy, *op. cit.*, p. 265.
24 Ben. M. Hall, *The Best Remaining Seats*, New York: Bramhall House, 1961, pp. 8–10.
25 Huntly Carter, *The New Theatre and Cinema of Soviet Russia*, London: Chapman and Dodd, 1924, p. 239.

CHAPTER SIX

1 Stephen Graham, *Changing Russia*, London: John Lane The Bodley Head, 1913, p. 92.
2 J. Leyda, *op. cit.*, p. 69.
3 W. K.-L. Dickson, *The Biograph in Battle*, London: T. Fisher Unwin, 1901, p. xiii.
4 Rachael Low, *op. cit.*, *1896–1906*, p. 67.
5 *ibid.*, p. 58.
6 *ibid.*, p. 59.
7 *The Cinema: Its Present Position and Future Possibilities*, *op. cit.*, p. 281.
8 B. Pares, *My Russian Memoirs*, London: Jonathan Cape, 1931, p. 485.
9 R. Bruce Lockhart, *Memoirs of a British Agent*, London: Putnam, p. 188.
10 Edgar Sisson, *One Hundred Red Days*, New Haven: Yale University Press, 1931, and G. Creel, *How We Advertised America*, New York: Harper Bros, 1920.
11 J. Leyda, *op. cit.*, p. 160.
12 *ibid.*, p. 138.
13 *ibid.*, p. 269.
14 E. H. Carr and R. W. Davies, *Foundations of a Planned Economy 1926–9*, London: Macmillan, 1969, p. 50.
15 Bertram D. Wolfe, *Kruschev and Stalin's Ghost*, London: Atlantic Press, 1957, p. 164.
16 J. Leyda, *op. cit.*, p. 268.
17 *ibid.*, p. 220.
18 P. French, *op. cit.*, p. 94.
19 Parliamentary Debates, 1927, Volume 203, Number 27, 2040.
20 *ibid.*
21 Sir Philip Cunliffe Lister, President of the Board of Trade, Parliamentary Debates, Volume 203, Number 27, 2040.
22 'Imperial Education Conference. Report of the Committee on the Use of the Cinematograph in Education', London: H.M.S.O., 1924, p. 19.
23 *The Times*, 19 January 1927.
24 B. Hampton, *A History of the Movies*, London: Noel Douglas, 1932, p.353.
25 Paul Leglise, *Histoire de la Politique du Cinéma Français. Le Cinéma et la Troisième République*, Paris: Pichon et Durand-Auzias, 1970, p. 70.
26 *The Times*, 18 September 1926.

27 Parliamentary Debates, Volume 203, Number 27, 2051.

28 *The Times*, 21 February 1922.

CHAPTER SEVEN

1 Reyner Banham, *Los Angeles. The Architecture of Four Ecologies*, London: Allen Lane, The Penguin Press, 1971, p. 35.

2 Louis Lochner (editor), *The Goebbels Diaries*, London: Hamish Hamilton, 1948, p. 165.

3 Alexander Walker, *op. cit.*, p. 105.

4 P. Mayersberg, *Hollywood the Haunted House*, London: Allen Lane, The Penguin Press, 1967, p. 73.

CHAPTER EIGHT

1 Alexander Walker, *op. cit.*, p. 212.

2 Kevin Brownlow, *The Parade's Gone By*, London: Secker and Warburg, 1968, p. 573.

3 Rachael Low, *op. cit.*, *1918–29*, p. 207.

4 Ernest Betts, *op. cit.*, p. 88.

5 *ibid.*, errata slip.

6 S. Eisenstein, *Film Form*, London: Dennis Dobson, 1951, p. 258.

FURTHER READING

In the 1920s hundreds of films were made in America and Western Europe but very few books about the cinema were published. During the 1960s and 1970s this situation has been completely reversed. Today people write about films instead of making them. Many of the books are of limited value and appeal only to enthusiasts with an insatiable appetite for details about stars and directors. The titles listed below are recommended as the most useful works published in English.

Towards a Sociology of the Cinema (Routledge, 1970) by I. C. Jarvie contains an excellent annotated bibliography of books and articles. Jarvie himself makes a number of interesting observations on the ways in which a sociologist might examine the behaviour of film-makers, film audiences and critics. *The World Encyclopedia of Film*, edited by T. Caukwell and J. M. Smith (Studio Vista, 1972), is a useful reference book.

The best and most recent general history of the industry is D. Robinson, *World Cinema: A Short History* (Eyre Methuen, 1973). This is especially good on the silent cinema and is written by a film critic who has a rare understanding of political, social and cultural changes outside, as well as inside, the studios and picture palaces. Robinson supersedes the earlier general outlines of R. Griffith and A. Mayer, *The Movies* (Simon and Schuster, NY, 1963), still the best illustrated introduction, and A. Knight, *The Liveliest Art* (Macmillan, NY, 1957).

T. Ramsaye's *A Million and One Nights* (Simon and Schuster, NY, 1926) is the source book from which so many later narratives have been quarried. Many of Ramsaye's errors and half-truths have been exposed by subsequent more scholarly writers, but his book retains the enthusiasm and excitement of a man who was involved in the very early days of the medium.

E. Wagenknecht, *Movies in the Age of Innocence* (Norman, Oklahoma, 1962), and G. C. Pratt, *Spellbound in Darkness* (Rochester, 1966), also recapture the primitive, improvised spirit of the early American cinema.

Among the many introductions to the craft of film-making and the principles on which films should be studied and evaluated, the following are recommended. I. Montagu, *Film World* (Penguin, 1964), is an exciting book written by one of the men who has done most to advance the cause of the cinema in this country. E. Lindgren's unpretentious but very informative *The Art of the Film* (Allen and Unwin, 1948) explains many basic facts about the history and the technicalities of cinematography.

Numerous studies of the cinema in individual countries have been published. A pioneer but still indispensable work is L. Jacobs, *The Rise of the American Film* (Harcourt Press, NY, 1939). D. Robinson's *Hollywood in the Twenties* (A. Zwemmer, 1968) recreates the happiness and self-confidence of America before the Depression. J. Leyda, *Kino: A History of the Russian and Soviet Film* (Allen and Unwin, 1960) is a more serious text on a more serious theme, a definitive work by the greatest English-speaking authority on the subject.

Pride of place, however, in the history of national film industries must be given to the four volumes of R. Low's *The History of the British Film 1896–1929* (Allen and Unwin, 1948–71). These are models of scholarship and understanding.

Few of the studies of individual directors or film stars are very satisfying. M. Seton's biography of *S. Eisenstein* (The Bodley Head, 1952) and R. M. Henderson's *D. W. Griffith: His Life and Work* (Oxford University Press, NY, 1972) fortunately deal effectively with these two major figures. No biography worthy of Chaplin has been written. His own *My Autobiography* (The Bodley Head, 1964) gives only tantalizing glimpses of his early life and studio career. R. Blesh has produced a devoted study of *Keaton* (Secker and Warburg, 1967).

We still await an economic history of the movie industry. Parts of the story, but only the American story, can be pieced together from M. Conant, *Anti-Trust in the Motion Picture Industry* (University of California Press, 1960), M. Huettig, *Economic Control of the Motion Picture Industry* (Philadelphia, 1944), H. T. Lewis, *The Motion Picture Industry* (Van Nostrand, NY, 1933), B. Hampton, *A History of the Movies* (Noel Douglas, 1932) and G. Jobes, *Motion Picture Empire* (Hamden, Conn. 1966). P. French, *The Movie Moguls* (Weidenfeld and Nicolson, 1969), summarizes the careers of the leading figures in the industry.

Even less has been written on the political role of the movies. L. Furhammer and F. Isaakson in *Politics and Film* (Studio Vista, 1971) examine some First World War and early Soviet material but quickly move on to the 'talkie' era. The sociology of film has also been neglected, largely because so little material exists from which an assessment of the influence of the cinema on social attitudes can be recreated. Jarvie concentrates understandably on the more recent period. However, two first-class studies of cinema architecture have been made. B. M. Hall, *The Best Remaining Seats* (Potter, NY, 1961) captures the great American houses, and D. Sharp, *The Picture Palace* (Hugh Evelyn, 1969) does the same for British and a few Continental theatres.

N. M. Hunnings, *Film Censors and the Law* (Allen and Unwin, 1967) not only summarizes the development of censorship in most major countries, but also throws light on many other aspects of film-making and exhibition.

An interesting literary approach is N. Vardac's *Stage to Screen* (Harvard University Press, 1949), an examination of the relationship between late 19th- and early 20th-century dramatic conventions and the development of a film narrative style.

Finally mention must be made of the best single book on the silent cinema, K. Brownlow, *The Parade's Gone By* (Secker and Warburg, 1968), a delightful collection of pictures and interviews with stars, directors, cameramen, stunt men and others involved in the birth of the movies. Read *The Parade's Gone By* and you are carried back into the uncomplicated magic of Hollywood in the 1920s.

INDEX

INDEX TO PRINCIPAL PROPER NAMES

INDEX TO FILM TITLES

8 9 2 4

30